Hidden in Plain Sight

Hidden in Plain Sight

Esther and a Marginalized Hermeneutic

Robert P. Debelak Jr.

WIPF & STOCK · Eugene, Oregon

HIDDEN IN PLAIN SIGHT
Esther and a Marginalized Hermeneutic

www.wipfandstock.com

ISBN 13: 978-1-4982-5067-2

This effort is humbly dedicated
to the One hidden among us in plain sight.

Contents

Preface

THIS ANALYSIS of a biblical narrative is intended for readers of English translations of Old Testament scripture[1] (knowledge of Hebrew or Greek not required). It gears toward raising an awareness of what is present and absent in a select text. Using the book of Esther, a prospective shape for a reading method is advanced to introduce examination of biblical story.[2] Tracing Esther's character, actions, and speeches is one entry into a story world; her role proposes a reading with sensitivity to the general components of Old Testament narrative and an appreciation for the text's literary art.

A brief overview on the power and construction of narrative begins the discussion. General comments review: a need for reading biblical narrative, a function of biblical stories, a research focus, and a sketch of developing the case for this reading model. The overview elaborates on the selection of the Esther story as representative of this proposed reading method, identifying four movements for engaging this literary genre in scripture. Stemming from the story of Esther (and informing the structure of this entire work), this approach involves: an awareness of self (backgrounds),

1. *Old Testament* is used out of respect for the time-honored status of this formative literary collection. The regard this esteemed body of literature is held in by the Judeo-Christian faith traditions bespeaks its contribution to life, faith, and ethic.

2. Readers unfamiliar with definitional aspects of biblical narrative are referred to works by Amit, Bar-Efrat, Alter, Fewell, Ryken, and the Mickelsens, to name only a few helpful resources. Full bibliographic citations appear at the end of this work.

searching the text (making observations), seeking meaning (interpretations, options, and implications), and living learned values.

A reading of Esther is supplied in chapter 2 with sensitivity to the narrative features of the text: narrator, characters, plot, space (setting), time, and style. The text is outlined in four major movements of character development that correlate with the above cited major components: Introduction, Crisis, Action, and Solidarity. To maintain the integration of narrative features, subsections of discussion relate titles and themes via comparison and contrast.

While historical-critical readings are needful and play an important part in the apologetic quest for truth, the potential to value the beauty and power of the story itself can be overlooked. Astute literary-critical analysis is a helpful companion in the reading journey, and based on Esther's example, may critique, but not (purposely) dethrone, other reading practices. Intentional inclusion of literary analysis in reading commitments is like Esther—the contribution is made when brought from periphery to center, beauty is recognized, and when the objective to lead readers in a positive direction (toward life) is acknowledged.

A brief summation prepares for discussion of select findings (implications). A case for reading biblical story asserts narrative features are present before readers; however, if ignored or if readers fail to discern these elements of biblical story, the delightful impact of biblical narrative remains hidden in plain sight, awaiting future discovery. The challenge is to learn an effective reading method of this genre—a method that does not neglect Esther (or narrative readings) in one's commitment to the study of scripture. Sources used in this work appear in footnotes and bibliographic citations. A separate section of supplemental resources is also included.

Three appendices offer practical illustrations for students to compare their own work with: *Appendix 1—Study*

Questions on the Text of Esther provokes thought and discussion relative to the reading in chapter 2. *Appendix 2—Framing Observations* identifies key features/facts of a text. Findings from Esther chapter 1 are framed as: declaration of finding, supporting discussion, and appropriate documentation. Emphasis is on *observation* rather than on *interpretation*. *Appendix 3—Compiling Narrative Observations* categorizes findings, illustrated by isolation of a particular narrative component. The element of "setting" from Esther chapter 1 demonstrates development of one aspect of this study (included in chapter 2, a reading of Esther).

Acknowledgments

As a faculty member of Lee University, Cleveland, TN, I am fortunate to be encouraged in my spiritual journey by family, friends, a faith community, and fellow faculty committed to academic excellence and partnership in quality Christian ministry. The giftedness of others sharpens my own awareness of who I am as a reader and as a teacher.

Dr. Terry Johns, Church of God Theological Seminary, is a constant friend, insightful colleague, and faithful dialogue partner; your passion for theology and people challenge me to see the importance of those marginalized in our world. Dr. Cheryl Bridges-Johns, Church of God Theological Seminary; thanks Cheryl, for helping me see the text more clearly. Dr. Jackie Johns, pastor, New Covenant Church of God; thank you for the encouragement to study and teach the Word of God in a ministry context.

I am grateful for the guidance in my doctoral program project (2003) rendered by Dr. Kathleen O'Connor of Columbia Theological Seminary; Kathleen, thank you for introducing me to the biblical Esther and for your dedication to excellence in scholarship. I offer a word of thanks to Dr. Paul Conn, President, Lee University, for his commitment to quality education and for his investment in the faculty of Lee University.

The friendship of Dave and Sue Griffith, Doyle and Brenda Howard, and students of Lee University is a gift beyond words. My parents, Robert (deceased) and Eilene

Debelak, and my brothers, David and Patrick, and their families, support me in their love and prayers.

Most of all, to my wife, Gudrun, and my sons, Bobby, Daniel, and Micah, thank you for your love and support. Your encouragement is a significant reason for this work coming to fruition.

1

Biblical Story

"A good story is irresistibly persuasive."

—Yairah Amit[1]

A Need for Reading Biblical Narrative

THE PROCLIVITY to tell story is part of human experience. Ask someone to rehearse the events of their day, and the response is a "story." Jokes are told as "funny stories." Eager listeners tune in to hear "personal and political stories." Readers flock to newsstands for the latest international "story." Daily interaction occurs as personal traits engage a world of change. Conflict pinnacles and subsides; it mounts or is resolved. How one tells the story of their life says much about their worldviews and coping skills. People communicate effectively in narrative forms. In short, we are narrative beings; we like a good story and we like to tell good stories.

What makes a story "good"? What riveting features of a saga glue one's attention to the pages of a text? Subjective responses vary with personal taste; but a gripping story line and the style by which a story is conveyed acknowledge the background and shaping of *protagonists* (heroes, heroines) and *antagonists* (villains) readers can identify with.

1. Amit, *Reading Biblical Narratives*, 2.

Audiences interface with the actions, emotions, challenges, etc., of the characters in their contexts. These experiences build a platform for sympathy, empathy, emulation, and the like. The more one can see herself or himself in the manners, celebrations, and struggles of the characters, the more an individual reader "enters the world of the story."

Given the penchant to good story, intentional ministry opportunity exists for Christian education emphases to foster reading the Bible as narrative. Raising a reader's sensitivity to the presence of narrative genre (and its qualities) in the Bible is the focus of this work. As narrative beings, knowledge and analysis of narrative components heighten appreciation for the prose elements of scripture. Heightening this awareness, however, is not without challenges.

In an era exhibiting less than optimum biblical literacy rates,[2] the diminished capacity to appreciate Holy Writ is in part due to a reader's unfamiliarity with what to look for in stories of the Bible. Passing acquaintance with general content of a few Bible stories may be present at varying levels in any given ministry setting, yet it is becoming rare to hear substantive discussion from pulpit, pew, or pupils on the components and crafting of biblical story. Culturally conditioned readers can demonstrate a general interest in "good story," while projecting a largely obscure awareness of their appreciation for the specific qualities of that story. Reflective of Stone and Duke's "embedded theology,"[3] a framework of presuppositions becomes more meaningful as basic assumptions are subjected to greater and more deliberate scrutiny. Thus, a general appreciation for good story may be acknowledged, but concrete commitments of reading

2. Van Wijk-Bos, *Ruth and Esther*, 7; see also Barna's June 14, 2005 report, "Christians Say They Do Best at Relationships, Worst in Bible Knowledge," a self-estimation of survey participant's biblical literacy levels and spirituality.

3. Stone and Duke, *How to Think Theologically*, 28.

remain veiled in one's personal analysis. To help alter this, a schematic is sought that will empower readers to identify, comprehend, analyze, and evaluate a text for personal and corporate meaning.[4]

Function, Power, and Biblical Stories

The presence of biblical stories testifies to the perpetuation of memories belonging to one era or group, providing a sense of identity, testimony, and historical continuity for subsequent generations of diverse audiences. One generation learns from another as telling "the story of the past is a mechanism for coping with exile and disruption."[5] For readers inheriting these narratives, the biblical stories entertain while simultaneously evoking response. The scrutiny of biblical narratives "reads the reader," and among many possible outcomes, imparts social mores, questions ethics, and offers character skills to deal with life. Readings elicit reactions that critique or inform the status quo, personal perspectives (faith, social, political, etc.), and the like.

These bare functions of story are relevant to contemporary Christian faith communities seeking to understand ancient biblical narratives for devotion and doctrine:

> The theological viewpoint that Christians form in the course of the life of faith is a distinctive set of many views, each relating in one way or another to the Christian message of God. Exactly what that message means is of primary concern to those seeking to understand their faith. In the church its substance is transmitted from generation to generation by means of

4. The relationship of learning levels or critical thinking emphases, as illustrated in Bloom's taxonomy, is in view.

5. Goldingay, *Israel's Gospel*, 697.

> the language of faith, a loose-knit collection of stories and symbols.[6]

As theology and worldviews (for these communities) are often shaped and reframed through perceptions derived from chosen passages of scripture, it is incumbent upon these audiences to be intentionally aware of the genre they are reading, and the reading methods they employ. As sacred, authoritative literature, sensitivity to biblical genre and its respective components offers fruitful ground for consideration in the quest for spiritual meaning:

> The distinction between the Bible as literature and the Bible as scripture is largely artificial. The church can properly hear its Bible as scripture only when it reads it as literature.[7]

This risky venture is open to the critique of whether or not one imposes modern tools of literary analysis on an ancient story or if the reader studies a text inductively seeking to read/hear the material on its own merits.[8] Biblical[9] narratives construct written worlds open to exploration through a variety of portals (or entries into that story world). Biblical narratives creatively integrate a narrator's telling of story through a variety of characters (each who embody and reflect numerous traits), scenes and settings, challenges, reversals (setbacks), irony, triumphs, and the like. The Bible captures these human experiences in this means of literary communication, blending these compo-

6. Stone and Duke, 29.

7. Clines, "Story and Poem," 115.

8. Craig's review of Bakhtin's argument: the Esther story shares traits in common with other ancient literature (see *Reading Esther: A Case for the Literary Carnivalesque*).

9. *Bible* and *biblical* are used in the Judeo-Christian sense of canon or sacred literature.

nents (and more) to offer case studies of a sort,[10] for readers to explore beliefs, motives, and ethics. In this way, the biblical story is a mirror for reflection. The biblical story world (potentially) becomes a vicarious arena of self-expression, where story characters and the complexities of their persona form a significant platform for analyzing what is esteemed or neglected among confessing Christians:

> In general, the biblical story is designed to enable us to discover who we are. We do that by telling our own story . . . in the context of the Bible story. We find ourselves by setting ourselves in that other story.[11]

Toward the interests of spiritual formation (experience and growth in Christ; a process informed by qualitative biblical study), a means of reading scripture is proposed in this work enabling students of the Bible to more intentionally observe the mechanics of biblical story. The means of reading advanced in this project are not a grid imposed upon scripture; rather, the paradigm stems from the structure and content of a selected biblical story itself.

Perspectives and Research Focus

Without claiming an objective-free perspective (bias) for reading, any particular lens impacts the potential for, and outcomes of, understanding a biblical story. To put it another way, how one reads either helps or hinders a close reading of the text. Understandably, *how* biblical narrative is read is the subject of various opinions, indicative of read-

10. Campbell observes, "The major attribute of a reader is the capacity to appreciate the artistry of the author or redactor, to spot the allusions to other threads in the biblical fabric. Authors and their products talk to us and meet our needs" ("Relishing the Bible," 813).

11. Goldingay, "Biblical Story and the Way It Shapes Our Story," 8.

ing commitments, pedagogical concerns, theological and political persuasions, educational goals, depth of learning, etc. Any two (from among many) selected reading models illustrates the potential polarized challenges for the modern reader, though the reading options (inclusive of both stress and depth) generally range from those disposed toward the rigors of intense analysis, to practices preferring casual or less serious levels of reading.

Defining a pole of reading commitments as a "less serious level" may be a critique surfaced by the demands of good scholarship. Without overgeneralizing, devotional readings often pegged in this category likely represent the largest segment of contemporary readers in the North American, English-speaking context. Bridging the gap between these two camps (scholarly and devotional) is, in part, the goal of quality Christian ministry. In an entertainment age inundating readers and viewers with a plethora of "story" in various forms (literary and dramatic), the trained observer (student of scripture), who is called to responsible Christian leadership, finds an initial gateway into valuable, age-appropriate, and reader-experience (appropriate) dialogue on the basis of the literature itself. This work advances the idea that the text itself offers the primary platform for a method that invites readers to glean the benefits of exploring and appreciating biblical narrative.

Regarding more intense forms of biblical study, a cursory glance reveals inclination (in our era) toward the influential historical-critical camp.[12] It is conceded that grounding texts in real time periods is a vital and apologetic goal of solid historical-critical work; this is a valuable component in the quest for meaning, and an appreciated disci-

12. Segovia's work, for example, surveys three biblical study methods critiquing historical criticism's sway over literary-critical and social-critical readings (*Decolonizing Biblical Studies: A View From the Margins*).

pline assisting in the differentiating between texts deemed part of a time-honored canon versus the spurious. However, the literary crafting and power of biblical story itself may be less evident or devalued if historical minutiae are the sole goal of scholarship.[13] This outcome may be less the fault of the discipline itself, and more indicative of any particular reader's choice. At the risk of undue segregation between the fields of biblical criticism and biblical story,[14] a practical balance is sought that facilitates greater admiration of the latter as part of the entire reading schematic.

Balancing the contributions reading commitments make to informed Christian ministry naturally stresses the need for careful literary analysis. Motivated by observation on practical ministry interests where the largest segment of Christian readership resides, literary-critical analysis brings to the process of biblical research a vital connection between heart and head in the reading experiences of diverse audiences. This angle of discussion, however, should not be construed to mean historical-critical interests have been abandoned.

I further concede these reflections stem from my context-specific and subjective experience. With Wesley's quadrilateral in mind (scripture, tradition, reason, and experience), the reflections in this work prioritize the scriptures themselves as the initial source of information to draw upon. This is the hub of this particular examination. Whole

13. Ibid. Kallai also discusses this concern in biblical and literary history ("Biblical Historiography and Literary History," 339). The contributions of historical-critical readings are not denied (Goldingay, "Biblical Story," 5), but moving past entrenchment in a single method of reading fosters inclusion of supplemental reading methods to augment research. See also, Sailhammer.

14. Harvey sees the dichotomy as largely artificial (*A Handbook of Theological Terms*, 42–44). Ideally, contemporary readings are to represent a balance in appreciation for the historical as well as for the literary features of a text.

works can be undertaken on various traditions of interpretation (scholarly commitments, faith-based lenses, etc.), as well as hermeneutical issues (philosophical interests stemming from or brought to a reading of the text). My concern though is to ask, "What can be gleaned from an analysis of a selected biblical passage and genre that sheds light on a potential reading method of scripture?"

Summarizing a Case for Reading Biblical Narrative

Our culture evinces a commitment to diversion where the most popular authors, actors, and actresses are applauded. Trivia buffs recite details of the hottest movie release. Excited engagement with the details of biblical story, however, is comparatively lacking. "Familiarity" makes an impact, so that in terms of practical application, diminishing interest in a biblical story is partly due to a reader's assumption of already knowing the story. Ignorance of what to look for accounts in some measure for the lack of "catch" or "hook"[15] to draw readers into a biblical story with equal interest as does the latest secular novel or drama. Yet, direct engagement with a biblical narrative and discovery of key components of the story's construction appeal to the narrative qualities of human communication, inviting detection of the building blocks of story—elements of communication readers are (unknowingly) familiar with. A guiding force of this work, then, is to observe what a text says (and how it says it) before asking what it means. This commitment prioritizes analysis before interpretation. This work asserts awareness of a biblical narrative's components leads to greater admiration for the apparatus and crafting of a story, enhancing

15. Richards and Bredfeldt, *Creative Bible Teaching*, 151–65.

one's potential for exploring a text's message, meaning, and relevance to contemporary life and ethic.[16]

Reading methods impact potential self-discovery and bear on the quality of ministry, requiring careful assessment of biblical literature prior to arguing for theological stances or interpretive outcomes. In making observations, appraising the content of biblical books distinguishes (for discussion) the *how* (poetics) from the *what* (meaning) of a text, where poetics is concerned with the "artistic dimension or the way the text is constructed."[17] With a text's artistic character in mind, Brueggemann asserts rhetorical criticism is "a method that insists on *how* what is said is crucial and definitive for *what* is said."[18] Further, "In terms of theological interpretation, because the *what* is linked to the *how*, one cannot generalize or summarize but must pay attention

16. *Discovery* of a chosen biblical text's components shapes this approach, where *meaning* and/or *application* are negotiated and contextualized only after engagement with the text of scripture itself. Readers may be interested in issues regarding where meaning is found. Duval and Hays, for example, summarize this tension by noting polarized camps suggest a text takes on its meaning only when the reader assigns such meaning (reader response) versus those positions favoring a view where the writer has in mind a meaning to convey (authorial intent) (see *Grasping God's Word*, 176). Campbell's assessment of author, text, and reader is also interesting: "When we think through what happens when we meet a text, we are likely to give priority to one or two of those ingredients. . . . What deconstruction does is give priority to the reader" ("Relishing the Bible," 813). At some level, the Esther text asserts the concept that regardless of reader response, the edict still called for the death of the Jews. There was meaning already intended, whether or not readers accepted that meaning. Esther's dialogue in community with Mordecai (Esth 4) is an important feature calling readers to a close and accurate reading to grasp the message conveyed by the author.

17. Osborne, *Hermeneutical Spiral*, 154.

18. Brueggemann, *Theology of the Old Testament*, 54.

to detail."[19] Hermeneutical options that diminish valuable reading methods may unduly influence research toward accrual of facts about texts, rather than inductively discovering features of the biblical story itself. The imbalance misses the congruity of literary art bound up in a text. By contrast, meticulous, accurate observations on the poetics of prose are antecedent to interpretive outcomes and inform this project first and foremost as a narrowed study of select English translations of a particular Old Testament text: the book of Esther.

Four Key Movements in the Book of Esther

"Neglect" or "oversight" of some biblical stories begs identification of ignored texts to illustrate a need for narrative studies and the positive contribution inclusion makes to research and reading commitments. This pedagogical concern detects biblical books and genre emphasized in a (local church or academic) curriculum, identifies biblical texts and genre neglected in the same program of study, and illustrates one suggestion toward inclusion of marginalized texts and genre in a family of research or Bible study courses. The Old Testament Esther is a representative of such underestimation. She is an orphaned Jewess living in exile, deemed a dominated member of a powerful society that manages its constituents. Yet she is the driving force of positive change transforming her world as an agent of life. The experiences of the story's heroine (Esther) integrate a reader's background, a written text, a struggle for meaning, and a posture of personal resolve. The dynamic combination of these four primary movements shapes the contours of an approach to reading biblical narratives.

19. Ibid., 55.

English translations offer access to the Masoretic (Hebrew) text, affording a means to peer into one possibility for reading a biblical narrative for a specific context of readers. This work will not entertain the later six Greek additions to the Esther scroll.[20] This analysis is an exercise offered under the rubric of observations "created," categorized, and compiled from the biblical text. While some interpretive outcomes will be explored, these interpretive results will not focus on questions of translation or on extensive text-critical matters; rather, the discussion capitalizes on outcomes pointing to a suggested reading method itself, and will be addressed only after engagement with the biblical story of Esther. These outcomes do not pretend to be exhaustive, nor the last word in any case; findings rather rest upon observations made on the story itself. If readers are prompted to the discovery of additional observations, or even critique, this effort will have been worth the journey. As a map to the design of this project, the artistic dimensions of the book of Esther will first be noted. A model for reading biblical stories (a model derived from the narrative of Esther itself) will subsequently be shown.

Esther's introduction, character development, actions, and speeches are traced as one entry into a specific story world. Her background, engagement with a written text, wrestling with meaning(s), and resolve to act represent four key movements of a biblically informed hermeneutic. The literary features in this story serve as one example for readers of Christian ministry contexts to explore the components, crafting, and clout of biblical stories. This reading method reacts to imbalanced study methods and the absence of specific Old Testament books from regular Christian reading commitments. As Esther is underestimated in her story world, narrative studies in Christian ministry contexts are

20. Note Levenson's commentary on *Esther*.

at risk of minimalization in curriculum or program design. Yet, as Esther is confronted by a text, her character transformation models a reading method for students of scripture. The Esther story shows how curricula can intentionally complement dominant study methods with literary-critical readings, in pursuit of theological formation.[21]

Exegesis Versus Eisegesis

A tension confronting contemporary readers, whether acknowledged or not, is determining if one's approach to a biblical story is (1) to "read in" to the text in order to find support for what one already believes (or wants to believe); or (2) open to the scripture's "reading out" its own message(s) and informing a reader's theology. When reading, Craig contends, "the past can never be condensed, closed, or hegemonized in meaning,"[22] while Amit distinguishes *eisegesis* (reading into) from *exegesis* (reading out of):

> The Sages said that the Bible has seventy faces, or aspects, but that is not to say that they are all equally valid. Some faces illustrate what the story's interpreters wish to find in it, while others shed light on the integration of the story's components. The reader should be able to distinguish between interpretations that serve the needs of interpreter and his/her readers and interpretations that strive to remain faithful to

21. Amit cites Weiss' "literary synchronic approach, as opposed to the dominant historical diachronic one; it ignores the history of the text and its stratification, and concentrates on the story's meaning in relation to its formal design" (12). See also Dillard and Longman, *An Introduction to the Old Testament*, 96–97.

22. Craig, 20.

> the significance that arises from the fashioning of the story.[23]

Though an entirely objective reading cannot be assumed, developing skills in analyzing biblical narrative increases the potential for acquiring informed hermeneutical practices. As a reader, one is not called to forsake one's identity under the assumption an objective examination of a text will result. Rather, one may "read" or be "read by" the text, where one's character makeup, skills or deficiencies, presuppositions, and the like are defined, coming under the scrutiny of engagement with a text. A reader's perspective is in turn subject to community dialogue. The challenge for meaning will then rest on a foundation of accurate, inductive observations on the writing, and lead to a call for commitment (putting what is learned into practice).

Esther models these elements as an "alien"; she is a woman in a male-dominated world and a Jewess displaced from geographic Israel. Yet, she (1) has a personal story held in relief to a larger story line; (2) engages a crucial piece of writing; (3) struggles in community with desired and realistic meaning(s) of an edict (see Amit above); and (4) resolves to act in solidarity with, and on behalf of, others subject to oppression.

Moving Toward a Reading of Esther

This reading will suggest one means for local Christian education curricula to consider in movement toward theological commitments, social concerns, or other research and ministry implications emerging from the study of scripture. To that end, literary analysis bridges historical-critical interests and a lived theology. While the valuable contributions of historical-critical readings are not intended to be

23. Amit, 137.

undermined, for the present, an emphasis will be placed on literary-critical issues. In part this emphasis is motivated by an observation that reading the text itself is the primary juncture into the field of biblical criticism.

The next segment offers a reading of English text(s) of the MT Esther,[24] with a literary-critical focus on her character development. Chapter 3 summarizes this reading's methodology, distilling particular findings. The final segment reflects on the general need for development of classes, courses, and conversation groups in reading biblical narrative. Appendices offer limited illustrations of the process itself.

24. Scripture references are from the King James Version and *New International Version.* Using English translations does not minimize translations used by international students or readers; rather, a common translation available to all students in the particular, primarily English-speaking contexts of this project is sought. Lack of familiarity with Greek or Hebrew by general-studies undergraduate students or non-discipline majors suggests an approach of introduction for a wide spectrum of readers in a particular ministry context.

2

A Reading of Esther

"From Victimization to Vindication"

ACKNOWLEDGING A text's multivalent nature is not new to biblical studies, and readings of the Esther story abound: Brenner's anthology of feminist essays,[1] Fox's character sketches,[2] and Mosala's social critique[3] represent only a few of many available readings. Textual concerns raise the number if the six Greek additions to the Esther scroll are considered[4] (though this is beyond the scope of this particular work). In terms of design, intent, function, or agenda, Craig argues the story of Esther is an early illustration of Bakhtin's "carnivalesque,"[5] where hilarity deconstructs hegemonious practices.[6] As a springboard for this interesting element and possible purpose of a story, Brenner comments, "Humor can be . . . didactic, a great aid for living and teac-

1. Brenner ed., *A Feminist Companion to Esther*, Judith and Susanna.

2. Fox, *Character and Ideology in the Book of Esther.*

3. Mosala, "The Implications of the Text of Esther," 1.

4. Levenson, *Esther.*

5. Craig, *Reading Esther.*

6. Bakhtin contends the experiences of folk culture (recorded in the literature) are derived from conflict with the official culture (Craig, 35). Thus, carnivalesque emerges in history when decentralization of a culture has undermined the authority of social establishments, national myths, and correct languages (Ibid., 37).

ing."[7] Through the means of humor, character interaction in this story segues to critiquing the status quo, for "authors of this genre are interested in representing the unusual and abnormal states of men and women—In what Bakhtin calls 'passions bordering on madness.'"[8]

While the above sampling is hardly comprehensive, various readings of the *Megillah*[9] posit this look at the Esther story as *a* reading and not *the* final word on this Old Testament book. An immediate presupposition is confessed in acceptance of this text as part of the Jewish and Christian canons;[10] as such, I will not explore questions of historicity at this time. That is a vital, but separate work in itself, and much has already been devoted to this topic by many able scholars. The general practice, though, of Christian education efforts is to first read a biblical text and then entertain questions of a historical nature. Thus, getting at a faithful reading of the narrative is a proposed initial step in this reading process, and is the focus of this particular discussion. Readers may be of any age group; with varied reading experiences, diverse levels of literary appreciation, and with text/story familiarity (biblical literacy) falling anywhere along a large spectrum of measure. Yet all readers, to

7. Brenner, "Obtuse Foreign Ruler," 40.

8. Craig, 40.

9. Kolatch, *The Jewish Book of Why*, 273; Glustrom, *The Language of Judaism*, 343–44.

10. Respect is given to the annual use of the Esther scroll during Jewish observances of Purim. By contrast, van Wijk-Bos observes the Esther story is largely neglected in Christian study and devotion (*Ruth and Esther*, 7). The absence of the Esther scroll in the Dead Sea collection is further an argument from silence on inclusion (or not) in a sectarian canon. Vermes states the absence of the text is "purely accidental," hinting that Aramaic fragments may form a proto-Esther of sorts (*The Complete Dead Sea Scrolls in English*, 11–12). Pages 578–79 of the same work emphasize these fragments serve only as a model and are not the canonical text of Esther.

greater or lesser extent, bring something of themselves to the text. So while one may or may not be aware of historical settings or issues, focusing on the story itself is a fine place for readers to start![11] The common ground of the text is the platform from which analysis will begin.

Beginning with the text poses several challenges for the contemporary reader, among which is a "distance"[12] between the reader and the events a text speaks of. Further concerns are related to the event(s) that may have motivated the writing of the story itself.[13] In terms, though, of the narrative's

11. Sailhammer aptly surveys the "presentation" of Old Testament theology in three ways—systematic categories, historical views, and central themes—In *Introduction to Old Testament Theology* (20). Of note, Sailhammer records the position of literary critics who charge that undue emphasis on purely historical methods of reading and research may neglect sensitivity to the awareness of literary features of the text: "By insisting on a purely historical approach to the presentation of an OT theology, it might be argued that other features of the biblical texts, such as their sense of story, can too easily be overlooked."

12. Such "distance" implies a host of "unknowns." Brueggemann comments that rather than risky engagement with a text, "distancing" in our contemporary era has become the very mask of scholarship some hide behind in the name of (objective) historical-criticism; (*Theology of the Old Testament*, 52).

13. This is not to say one abandons the historical context or historical forces impacting a text, nor is it to say that imposing contemporary literary practices is the final answer for work in biblical theology. Dillard and Longman caution against a temptation to emphasize the literary nature of a text to the neglect of historical forces related to, and impacting a text. They caution against assuming contemporary practices of literary analysis are in and of themselves an appropriate grid to impose on an ancient text (21). Later in their work, Dillard and Longman highlight how a synchronic approach to reading Old Testament texts focuses on how the text exists (final form) rather than reconstructing the alleged underlying sources or history of the text's composition and redaction (96–97). For this work on the book of Esther, the final form as we have it in modern

mechanics, "If we want to understand a text from a distant culture, we can—on a modern account—enter into the text's world on the basis of the humanity we share with the text's original authors and addressees,"[14] even if the author is unknown and the first audience remains obscure.[15] Insofar as a story's characters potentially become a narrator's/writer's (these do not have to be the same person[s]) mouthpiece, a story's characters represent an interface between the writer and the reader. Thus, tracing Esther's character development serves as a possible entry into this particular story world. Toward discovery of a reading schematic, I begin with the text of Esther itself and analyze the narrative's general components of literary art.

Overview of the Story of Esther

The Esther story is a saga of human struggle for survival against odds of imposed domination. This narrative rehearses resistance to abusive power in various arenas of so-

English translations of the MT Esther is the basis of discussion for readers of a select North American context. The contribution(s) of the historical-critical method(s) of reading is not abandoned, but may be supplemented and/or critiqued by inclusion of hearing the voice of literary criticism in research.

14. Adam, *What is Postmodern Biblical Criticism?* 8.

15. Brueggemann contends, "The primary point . . . is that Israelite faith is not a disembodied set of ideas, as Euro-American theology had assumed in its hegemonic innocence, but that this faith, like every statement of meaning, is deeply enmeshed in and shaped by material reality. . . . This means that the Old Testament . . . is in important ways, intimately and inexorably linked to lived reality" (*Theology of the Old Testament*, 51). Responding to Alter's work, Campbell further offers: "I hardly need to know the author by name or context; he or she is a trustworthy participant in our common human quest for meaning. I do though, need to relish the author's artistry. We certainly need such reminders that the Bible is magnificent literature" ("Relishing the Bible," 813).

cial challenge (gender and ethnic tensions). It deconstructs the oppressive controls of life through conflict and trials facing exilic Jews. In this account, a young Jewish woman confronts difficult issues in her move from near obscurity to prominence.[16] A familiar theological theme subtly hovers in the background ("from nothing to something"). As Esther delights (tames!?) foreign managers of the exile,[17] she simultaneously secures the safety of her people as they transition "from victimization to vindication." The David versus Goliath quality of overcoming mammoth opposition echoes on both personal and corporate levels.

A basis for thematic shifts is formed in Esther chapters 1 and 2, and is recast in new characters, events, and turnabout in chapters 3 through 10. This reading introduces and defines Esther's character (chs. 1–2); examines her reading of a written text surfacing her options for action (chs. 3–4); and explores her personal resolve to live in solidarity with others of like experience (chs. 5–10).

Character Introduction (Esther Chapters 1–2)

(Readers are encouraged to refer to the study questions for these chapters found in appendix 1.)

Esther's initial character sketch provides only scant detail generally describing the young orphaned Jewess. For

16. Various interpretive summaries celebrate victory (an etiology for Purim) or seek to account for omission of אל (el), אלהים (elohim), or יהוה (YHWH—the Tetragrammaton) in the text. Esther 4:14 may be a subtle reference for God's providential care, though Wiebe argues an alternative rendering of the passage questions, "Will help come at all?" (see "Esther 4:14: Will Relief and Deliverance Arise for the Jews From Another Place?").

17. Similarities exist in the Joseph and Esther stories: a Jewish hero/heroine finds favor in a foreign monarch's court, working to save their nation through wise service in Gentile environments.

all practical purposes, she is "sidelined." Yet readers are introduced to the "beautiful" Esther with no qualification of how "loveliness" is defined. Without specific clarification of her physical beauty, the power of imagination allows readers of any age to frame or define Esther's splendor without detraction from the story line. The text will rather stress the magnificence of her internal character and the nobility of her actions.

From another angle, the (intentional?) obscurity of her exterior attractiveness and focus on her integrity hints at a movement from social periphery to public center: she is ambiguous for readers; information about her specific age and a definition of pleasant appearance remain vague and open-ended for subjective, inventive construction.[18] She is present, yet hidden in plain view. It is clear, though, she is an alien in foreign territory (as a Jewess) and one subject to political hegemony (control) (female queen); yet it is this very "camouflage" that becomes the means by which she noticeably succeeds in an empire of oppression.

In a story of transposition (change), her personal background is explored against the narrative's opening scenes. Vashti's vital role is an introduction to the story, and identifies Esther with her precursor, the queen, Vashti.

FROM GREAT TO SMALL: THE STORY'S STAGE

The story's narrative art testifies "to literary skills of a high order;"[19] not "historical ineptness or naiveté," but "a rich context for irony, parody, and farce."[20] The Persian captivity forms the story's *Sitz im Leben* (setting in life), dovetailing

18. A point commensurate with Goldingay's and Adam's (prior) comments on contemporary readership's intersection with a text based on subjective human experience.

19. Gordis, Religion, *Wisdom and History*, 383.

20. Humphreys, "Story of Esther," 336.

on the Babylonian exile (2:6) as a raw reminder of dislocation from *eretz* Israel (the land of Israel). This crafting of the story's setting stages tones of shame and marginalization for implied audiences well versed in the experiences of *Diaspora* (exile). Xerxes' reign is cast as "powerful" in territorial and numeric terms (India to Ethiopia; and counting provinces) no less than fourteen times in the whole book (1:1, 3, 14, 19–22; 2:3; 3:8–15; 8:5, 9, 17; 9:2, 4, 12, 20, 30). Spatial details telescope from broad to local, allocating the Northeast to Southwest borders of the kingdom in tandem with a bold quantitative resume of "127 provinces" (1:1). These features introduce characters, create space in a known historical era, and commence an initiation of "readers to a world that is differently constituted from their own."[21]

The international mix (Persia and Media [v. 3]) and extended introduction of chapter 1 parade a barrage of masculine characters: King Xerxes, unnamed princes, chamberlains, wise men, servants, and "men" in general. Rendering *people* (*ha am*; העם [v. 5]) with the gender-charged term, *men*, is driven by the immediate context of masculine nouns and supposes females attend Vashti's later-mentioned feast "for the women" (v. 9).[22] The phrase "nobles and princes of the provinces" (v. 3 KJV) reinforces the hierarchical pecking order. Stress on masculinity advances lines of authority and power for the narrative's setting. The men's garden party is lavishly adorned in colorful detail (blue and white linens, purple material, silver, marble, gold, mother of pearl [v. 6]), a description of rich décor followed by the "king's command" that men drink liberally ("each . . . what he wished"

21. Amit, *Reading Biblical Narratives*, 33.

22. Levenson, *Esther*, 43; see interpretive notes in *The Talmud of Babylonia*, where XVII.N.1 reads "separate parties" for men and women (Neusner, 773). Craig includes choice for women in the festivity of drinking (54). My reading sees segregated drinking as a line of demarcation between the powerful and the powerless.

[vv. 7–8]).[23] The boundless outdoor stage of male revelry receives more narration time and space (eight verses), contrasting the single verse and "diminished mention" of Vashti's segregated indoor assembly ("for the women" [v. 9]).

During the six months ("180 days") of feasting (v. 4) and subsequent seven-day palace festivities (v. 5), Persia and Media (great and small) revel in hegemonious (power or control) success. The geographic horizon telescopes a vast empire to a local center in Susa. The slighter space given to female "festivity" in only a single verse (v. 9) reverberates "bigger to lesser"; moving from great to small, implying "superior to inferior." The women-only guest list, their indoor "celebrating," and the omitting of extensive details of their party setting underscores subjugation as verse 9 deflates the moment with the caveat (comment) that even the house is not the queen's; her banquet is held "in the royal palace of King Xerxes." The spatial prominence closing chapter 1 defines the empire once more with a "flexing of muscles" fitting for the machismo (male) power structures stressed directly and symbolically in the passage. This "marking of territory" sketches an immense kingdom as an essential framework for time sequences and character actions when the edicts are dispatched (1:19–22; 3:15; 8:7–14; 9:14). By

23. The story world is akin to another exilic event of an insensitive or dull-witted, foreign king (Brenner, "Obtuse Foreign Ruler," 42–43) feasting with wine, followed by judgment when the protagonist speaks. A reading of Daniel 5 finds: an exilic setting, wine feast, court setting, favor found, and writing (on a wall in Daniel; edicts in Esther), followed by judgment. The lion's den story further offers a similar structure of story elements: conspiracy, piety, irreversible law, victory, conspirator(s) put to death in the manner proposed for the hero, and a resolution of the conflict ending on a note of favor with the king. These components shape the respective structure of stories in each book, offering interesting comparison between the Daniel and Esther narratives.

creating this space (or stage for the story),[24] the narrative anticipates "reversal." Commensurate with Amit's comments about narrative features, change is inevitable; for without change, there would be no story.[25] The stage is set and ripe for turnaround, projected in the first conflict of the escalating plot—Vashti's challenge to the king's power base.

The Vital Role of Vashti

The story introduces the first of only three named women in the book—Queen Vashti. Her silent role repudiates (challenges) minimalization of females in the capitol (1:9–12). In an empire of opulence (affluence), King Xerxes summons her before the male partygoers. However, she refuses to be another of his trophies. Adeney's generalization of contemporary gender tension resonates in this biblical story: "When people are rich, women are valued as décor or as property."[26] Vashti's refusal to respond to the king's "invitation" is significant: "India to Ethiopia," 127 provinces, and palace grandeur may all be displayed for an ogled male mob, but she counters dehumanization and invasion of female space implicit in the official "male" command. Her rebuff of Persia's men defies submission to cultural expectation as an object on which the masculine managers of her society may gloat. While men toast their "power" (vv. 13–22), she will not condone their revelry as one more adornment of male conquest and boasting.

24. Beal argues for chapter 1's integral relationship to the rest of the narrative ("Tracing Esther's Beginnings," 103). If chapter 1 is segregated from the story, Esther's importance to the rest of the narrative is greatly diminished. Craig concurs; "An opening scene is always important to consider because it sets a tone for the entire narrative" (52).

25. Amit, 34.

26. Adeney, "Esther across Cultures," 333.

Seven named nobles (v. 14) expedite counteraction to her defiance, showing how one woman affects a whole kingdom. Oddly, she disobeys royal order, yet no existing regulation is cited (except "the command of the king" [v. 15 KJV]) to deal with her rejection of Xerxes' summons. Readers later learn that appearing before the king without invitation is subject to death (4:11); for now, rejecting invitations is equally not an option. Yet beyond the emotional perplexity, the king and court do not know immediately how to handle being *told* "no" by a woman. Thus, a special meeting convenes to deal with Vashti's insubordination and to draft a new law (1:15).[27]

Vashti's silent protest profoundly threatens Memucan, who perceives a feminist revolt will challenge a male monopolization of supremacy in the kingdom. After all, seven of Xerxes' men, possessing privileged, royal authority, are snubbed (rendered impotent!) by one woman's "no" (v. 12). Though her presence is brief, Memucan's resentment shapes Vashti's significance; he fears she is a trendsetter whose "conduct will become known to all the women, and so they will despise their husbands." Thus, he requires her replacement with a more domesticated figure (vv. 16–20).

27. Keil and Delitzsch soften "banishment" with "divorce," ("Esther," 301, 319), likely inferred in the separation of Xerxes from Vashti and "writing" after their union is publicly dissolved. It is unclear from the Esther story if this is Persian law and/or another influence on the text. That a "new law" is penned and dispatched indicates something not previously practiced is at work. Goldingay sees no execution of Vashti; rather, some form of "retirement" and her continued presence as a symbol of a feminist movement (*Israel's Gospel*, 780); this is difficult, considering the court's purpose for ridding the empire of Vashti to avoid any further influence by her. While the deportation, divorce, or death of Vashti are all possible, the point of the narrative is her successor, Esther, follows in her footsteps by mimicking Vashti's countercultural actions.

The court's input to this domestic matter is hilarious! Regal declaration hopes to overshadow Vashti's boldness by putting an official spin on a press release (vv. 19–22). The administration's inept effort to save face is sought through "banishment" or a ridding of her "dangerous memory."[28] An edict is issued (vv. 19–22) to offset "disrespect and discord" (v. 18) marring the empire's image, yet the first *diktat* (punitive settlement; authoritative statement) ironically informs Xerxes' realm of the very scandal Memucan wishes to quench![29] While "Queen Vashti" (vv. 9, 15, 17) is reduced to "Vashti" (v. 19), the story indirectly suggests a "weak" queen is shamed far less than a "powerful" king who is not even aware of the embarrassment he inflicts on himself and his kingdom by his personal airing of a private marital squabble to the far and public reaches of his empire.

Xerxes' *raison de'tre* (rationale) for the decree bolsters his position as male and as king. His act to rally men numerically infers there is no real justice for women. A large empire and male freedom in this story's crafting silently, but significantly, assert that "bigger is better," that "more equals power," and that "might is right." Ironically, empowering (the already powerful) men to rule their homes with imperial authority (v. 22) is a feeble swinging of control through quantitative means to Xerxes' side. The king's (and his council's) act of dehumanizing, dethroning, and dismissing Vashti seeks to exonerate a drunken monarch at the expense of another (in this case, a "weak" female). Yet, where gender and politics are concerned, authority alone cannot be the last word; power can be, and often is, abused.[30]

28. Florence, "The Woman Who Just Said 'No,'" 37.

29. Levenson, *Esther*, 51.

30. Characteristics of the "obtuse ruler" make some impact here (see Brenner and Van Wijk-Bos). Goldingay wittingly includes, "Authority makes stupidity more public and more dangerous" (*Israel's Gospel*, 780).

One woman rebuffs seven courtiers and a king, dismantling royal authority in a single, silent act. Her stance predicates (readies) the dissolve of male power constructs to come later in the narrative. In her actions, the female queen satirizes the male king as a protest of the disenfranchised: "To impute impotence to somebody potent and powerful is almost the only kind of revenge available to the impotent and powerless."[31] In this episode,

> Satire turns laughter into a weapon for moral reform rather than a toy for indulging pleasure. It combats corruption and injustice, stupidity, and delusion by means of a militant irony.[32]

Jones assumes "it is easier to bear pain or subjugation if one can mock those in authority or those responsible for the pain,"[33] suggestive of Goldingay's point that "the human imagination is able to overpower human history."[34] Yet, Vashti has no say, unless indirectly via the "voicing" of her plight through Xerxes' absurd "royal" edict! Void of place (v. 9) or voice of her own, any critique she offers must be accomplished vicariously (through another). Ironically, her lack of voice speaks loudly to (or by!) an otherwise outspoken male populace.

ESTHER—A QUEEN JUST LIKE VASHTI

A subtle, but significant point is couched in 2:4, where an obstinate queen loses title and office and a "better" woman is sought "instead of Vashti." Playfully teasing the phrase "instead of" implies more than just "one to take the place of another." *Instead* (or "in her stead") infers Esther is po-

31. Brenner, "Obtuse Foreign Ruler," 51.
32. Wood, "People Are Funny," 976.
33. Jones, "Two Misconceptions," 172.
34. Goldingay, *Israel's Gospel*, 778.

tentially "like" the former queen. For the court (of male power brokers), this phrase conveniently means "her place" as queen. However, the subtle wordplay readies readers for a dramatic unveiling of character: while Esther is in the office of queen formerly held by Vashti, her role "in her stead" plays out that she, like Vashti, will change things. This angle binds the countercultural actions of the first *koenigen* (queen), Vashti, to Esther's emerging character as an agent of change.

Selecting a (second) queen does not prevent a second gathering of virgins (v. 19). Like Vashti, they are exploited and without voice. Even Esther defers to Hegai; it is the narrator who artistically fills in the details (v. 15). These illustrations function to cast a stage where men of the kingdom assemble and control women, leaving Esther as little more than a figurehead; for men, she is a trophy for display—"instantly being made queen."[35] While Esther is superior in beauty (2:17), in this empire women are collectively inferior to men.[36] At her best, she is still held in check and dehumanized as a queen the kingdom would gloat upon and *man*-ipulate.[37]

Esther's ascent to the throne[38] is fraught with the theme of male oppression. The king selects his bride, but

35. R. Pfeiffer, "Esther," 479. Pfeiffer accents the immediate pleasure Xerxes took in this unique woman; his words should not be construed to compare her immediate "promotion" with that of Haman's in chapter 3. A key difference is Esther's ascent to the throne required a comparatively lengthy process (ch. 2), whereas Haman's promotion is without specified involvement of other characters, nor is any lapse of time intimated.

36. Craig, 93. Gender assignment immediately proposes women are "politically ineffectual." However, women in the Esther story effectively satirize the men and the social/political fabric of their settings (Brenner, "Obtuse Foreign Ruler," 46–48).

37. Emphasis intentional here and throughout the discussion.

38. Esther's marriage is controversial. A historical lens contends

the woman has no say. Women chosen by Persia's monarch have no real freedom (2:12–14; 4:11); they must await personal invitation to meet Xerxes.[39] Without a summons *by name*, females of Xerxes' world are nameless, faceless pawns. Esther, a woman subject to the penalty of violating this rule, will reference proscription ("law") against arbitrary meetings with Xerxes. Indiscriminate and uninvited audience with the king subjects one to the severest penalty; infractions of this protocol are terminal, as she warns: "the king has but one law: death" (see 4:11).

Shaping Esther "in Vashti's stead" thus fuses the two characters in rank as queens, but more in terms of their "likeness" or "how they are alike." Silenced and exploited like Vashti, Esther follows a court-defined role only so far before she too challenges the status quo. She, like Vashti,

---

Persian noble status is required, yet the story mentions no such requirement. Both queens are criticized from a patriarchal expectation that women obey men, or bear the stigma as violators of "law"; see Hambrick-Stowe's assumption that Vashti is "uppity" ("Esther the New Moses," 1132); or Goldman's "dominating" wife idea ("Narrative and Ethical Ironies," 17). Esther is condemned as unfaithful, for she, a Jew, marries a pagan (see Niditch in "Folklore, Wisdom, Feminism and Authority," 41; Levenson, *Esther*, 49). In Esther's defense, she is queen, but did not seek the rank. She admits little contest if her plight is due to slavery (7:4), and is willing to work in the sphere of this injustice. Branding her less than Jewish or dishonorable is unfair, missing the humanness of her struggle. It may also be a telling remark on contemporary readers who prefer the "beauty pageant" concept to her accessing the throne—a position I vigorously reject.

39. Women in this story remain in well-defined boundaries—Vashti in the king's house (ch. 1), Esther indoors (ch. 2), Zeresh at "her" home (5:10–14; 6:12–13)—though Vashti is a countercultural symbol, Esther an agent of deconstruction, and Zeresh an insightful woman foreseeing her husband's demise. Ironically, the exchanges between Haman and Zeresh reveal the inner life and thoughts of the story's nemesis (Craig, 66) in a series of events set into motion, all because one woman was feared (Ibid., 82).

will have far-reaching effect in the kingdom when delivering her people from death. While it is Xerxes' realm, Esther will be influential. Thus, Vashti's role informs Esther's part in refusing persecution to run its course.

This background is the first movement of how Esther's character is a model for Christian education efforts promoting the reading of biblical texts. The scant details of her heritage and appearance, as well as the creation of space as a politically charged environment of gender oppression, are factors of experience she brings to her reading of a text (ch. 4). Readers are told only that Esther is an orphaned Jewess whose upbringing has been under the auspices of a community-minded male, Mordecai. Even in her ascent to the throne, she is ordered by a man not to divulge her national background. It is safe to surmise she is a woman of obedient character. One can suppose the connection to a relative, Mordecai, implies her own affiliation with the tribe of Benjamin. She is described as beautiful, and both Hegai and Xerxes honor this quality (though suspiciously and for selfish reasons). Readers, though, must supply their own definition of beauty as they venture further into the book. Esther is now before readers, yet she remains obscure; hidden from concrete definition and hidden stylistically by her absence in chapter 3.

This absence of Esther in the next chapter is prepared for in chapter 1; like the women who party indoors (1:9), Esther too now has a place. Her place, though, is defined immediately in spatial terms (the kingdom's headquarters at Susa), but more inferentially defined and developed later in the story as queen "in Vashti's stead" (place or likeness). For a king and kingdom assuming an insular safety, their world is now settled—a queen is in place who will act more "responsibly" (in terms of a domesticated definition). The narrative thus takes readers to the edge of their seats and leaves them "hanging" for further development of this pivotal character's role in order to substantiate just how she, Esther, is like Vashti. Until then, a lingering question rightfully begins its echo: "Where is Esther?"

Character in Crisis (Esther Chapters 3–4)

(Readers are encouraged to refer to the study questions for these chapters found in appendix 1.)

Chapters 3 and 4 escalate the story's plot-tension as a crisis challenges Esther. She reads a document (crafted in chapter 3) and her idealistic responses to cloak reality (silence and excuses) are deconstructed in dialogue with Mordecai (chapter 4). Esther's reading of a document and her pondering of potential responses result ultimately in her resolve to intercede for others.

Marking this second movement in her character development is a reversal of the story's stage. The binding of Esther's character to a specific role and heritage are integral in her move from periphery to center. Whereas the narrative began with a theme of "From Great to Small," this theme reverses in chapters 3–4 to "From Small to Great." The first segment's emphasis on "The Vital Role of Vashti" paves the way for "The Vital Role of Mordecai" in relationship to Esther's anticipated actions. Finally, with Vashti's position fused to Esther's role as queen, national and religious connotations are bound up in casting "Esther as a Jew like Moredecai."

From Small to Great: Recasting the Story's Stage

The themes of chapters 1 and 2 advance the plot in chapter 3. Men enjoy liberality with wine and audience with the king (1:7–8). Haman's obscure proposal to eradicate the Jews (3:8–9) transpires in a context of men again gathering with wine (revisiting the familiar kingdom penchant of marginalization). While it may be court protocol, it is clear males of this story world enjoy much greater freedom: men are present in immediate council with the king, not women (1:13–22); Haman appears at will (6:5) (his office may extend him privileges, but readers are given no such information). Oddly, Xerxes[40] requires help deciding Vashti's fate and selecting a new queen (a woman) (chs. 1 and 2), but without hesitation or assistance he elevates Haman (a man) to "a seat of honor higher than that of all the other nobles" (3:1–2).

The story's nemesis, Haman, is irritated by Mordecai's refusal to honor him, and the two male characters are held in tension with each other; Haman the Agagite's shaping and role diametrically oppose the role and shaping of Mordecai the Jew. Haman subsequently visits Xerxes, generically requesting "to sacrifice a whole nation . . . to satisfy his personal hatred of one man."[41] Without (conveniently) identifying the victims, Xerxes and Haman strike a bargain, the king stating his royal interest in money matters rather than human life. The ease of Xerxes and Haman sitting and drinking contrasts the *dis-ease* of people subject to dismissal

40. Xerxes is caricatured as a "royal buffoon," indecisive with females and hiding behind "law" when called to spare Jews. He toys with people's lives, allows conflicting edicts, and lacks emotion when his subjects perish. He drinks, enjoys women, delegates responsibility, and taxes—acts of autonomy distancing him as an odd ruler in a kingdom of opulence. Brenner's "Obtuse Foreign Ruler" identifies consistent traits in biblical narratives shaping foreign monarchs as greatly inept (42–43). Talmon sees personification here of the witless king; an ideal "type," rather than an exact historic figure of Persia ("Wisdom," 441). He is a party animal, and at times a caring husband (though he likes women only as long as they please him). His complexity is seen in revelry, anger, despair, hospitality, etc; thus, he is the unrestrained, immoral playboy who lacks a moral compass (Levenson, *Esther*, 46), typed to offset Esther and Mordecai, who serve as a moral conscience in a lawless, selfish society.

41. Talmon, 448.

and death (like Vashti [1:19]; recast as the collective "city of Susa" [3:15]). The edict of chapter 1 prepares for the decree of chapter 3: in chapter 1 *man*-ipulation by Memucan announces Vashti's "offense" to the empire; likewise, Haman's scheming in chapter 3 incipiently revisits Vashti's banishment (ch. 1) in a kingdom-wide order for Jewish extermination (3:15; "removal" or "erasure").[42]

Stylistic affinity exists throughout the book as structure and theme keep readers in tune with the story line. This affinity is crafted in six consistent literary features from chapters 1–2, which repeat in subsequent scenes throughout the book as a whole: revelry, requirement, refusal, reaction, response, and reference.[43] These features invert in acts and through characters shifting power to loss and conversely exalting the humble. Personified in Mordecai, turnabout of personal challenge parallels the Jew's corporate victory, positing him as a transitional figure between Vashti's plight and Esther's bravery.

The Vital Role of Mordecai

Interaction with Mordecai appreciably shapes Esther's character.[44] He cares for the orphan, requiring she conceal her Jewish identity (2:7, 10), but he does not (or he is not able to) keep her from the harem (vv. 8–9).[45] The animos-

42. Beal, "Tracing Esther's Beginnings," 103–7.

43. See Chart A on pages 143–44.

44. The relationship between Mordecai and Esther is ambiguous: is she cousin, niece, or fiancée/wife? The latter raises serious ethical issues to which the narrative lends no insight. If, for example, Xerxes' edict calls for virgins, why would Mordecai send his wife? If she is full partner of a consummated relationship, this would make Mordecai complicit with Xerxes' oppression.

45. Contemporary readings are fascinated (enamored?) with the "beauty contest" idea. While our culture is accustomed to Miss America pageants, these voluntary events drastically differ from

ity between Mordecai and Haman may recall the ancient Saul-Agag drama,[46] but Esther appears to lack knowledge[47] of this historical tension (4:4). She, rather, is more startled by the condition of Mordecai's attire, and mediators carry messages between them (v. 5). Her new life as queen is cast as an existence of insulation and isolation,[48] framed further in her giving clothes to Mordecai (another act of insulation) and in her pondering to remain silent about her Jewish identity (v. 14).

Her gift of garments attempts to "cloak" reality in a self-defined idealism. Her life as queen fabricates an illusion of a safe existence in the veneer of fashion. Mordecai rejects

---

taking and preparing young girls for a king's "try before he buys" routine. The idea of "contest" is objectionable due to violation of "free choice;" a feature foreign to Esther 1 and 2. The episode is rather one of gender oppression, and perpetuating an illusion of a positive competition between "Barbie dolls" of the empire is to fall prey to the very hegemonial powers instituting the oppressive controls in the first place. While Goldingay suggests Esther begins her career as a "bimbo" (*Israel's Gospel*, 780), readers must not press the illustration too far. The text reveals little of Esther's emotional disposition toward this life, with the exception of her later plea before Xerxes: "If we had merely been sold as male and female slaves, I would have kept quiet" (7:4). Perhaps readers might consider (from the viewpoint of the unnamed and faceless virgins of Esther 2, as well as the perspective of Esther herself) that beauty was a curse in this context.

46. See Kallai's stages of "reutilization," "representative designation," and "altered presentation" of story ("Biblical Historiography," 341–42), and use of antecedent character principles as prototypes voiced by Talmon on Esther's role: "Biblical writers were fully aware of the ageless truth that strong and powerful men most easily are overcome by female cunning"—Samson, Siserah, and Abimelech (450–51).

47. The question of "Who lacks knowledge?" is raised at several points (see Bea Wyler, "Esther: The Incomplete Emancipation of a Queen," 125–26). Even readers are at times without knowledge as to the rationale behind the events (Levenson, *Esther*, 2).

48. Van Wijk-Bos, *Ruth and Esther*, 85.

her gift of "false security" (clothing), sending a "present" in return—a copy of Haman's death order (v. 8). He preempts her innermost thoughts before she can find an answer requiring no accountability to the text (v. 13). Dialogue in this "community" context shapes her response as she is held accountable by reminder she is Jewish and cannot escape the decree of death imposed by Haman's letter. Mordecai thus deconstructs her excuses, hinting *her* intercession may be the single most definitive factor in overturning the death threat (v. 14).[49]

Esther's trepidation is akin to Moses' anxiety of appearing before Pharaoh and making demands. She reasons against visiting the king; Xerxes is a ruler in this story who selects, schedules, and summons women (2:14). Invading male royal space incurs a death sentence; Esther's alarm states, "thirty days have passed" since her last call (4:11).[50] Haman is without anxiety when visiting Xerxes (5:14—6:5), yet Esther's appearing without summons risks death (4:16). Thus, her act of calling on the monarch challenges a domineering patriarchalism by crossing boundaries of limited, conditional female access to the king. She will ultimately forego her own sense of security, abandoning her life in the process. As a countercultural actress, her persona develops as queen "in Vashti's place" (see 2:4) and likeness.

49. Wiebe's comments and implications for readings here concern divine providence ("Esther 4:14"), asking the provocative question if "deliverance will come at all" if Esther does not act. Weiland's differing theological tack argues in favor of divine providence as a subtly veiled theme of "hidden yet present" in the book of Esther (see "Literary Clues to God's Providence," 34–47).

50. Yamauchi (Hoerth, Mattingly, and Yamauchi, *Peoples*, 117) thinks Esther's "not being called" implies Xerxes' absence, roughly correlating with a war against Greece or some other nation. The reason for not calling her is left unstated in 4:11, unless one infers the large harem (ch. 2) symbolizes she was not "needed."

Reading and dialoguing in community transform Esther. Mordecai fills in her lack of knowledge, holding her answerable to the edict's implications. While Xerxes also "lacks knowledge" (victim's identity) in this story (ch. 3), his refusal to repeal the execution order (3:13; 8:7–8) is more about his apathy toward human life.[51] The king hides behind wine and counselors; in contrast, Esther may not read *Time* magazine, but she is hardly indifferent. Under the threat of death and in the face of potential, immediate execution, she sheds "protection" ("safe" submission to royal managing [4:11]; and repression of her identity [2:10]), resolving to "go to the king" (4:16).

Esther—A Jew Just Like Mordecai

The plot mounts toward a pinnacle in the crisis, bearing on the significance of Esther's character. Reaching personal resolve—"If I perish, I perish" (4:16)—4:13–17 is "the turning point in Esther's development"; a scene in which her character

> . . . moves from being a dependent of others (all of them men) to an independent operator who, whatever the objective restrictions on her freedom, will work out her own plans and execute them in order to manipulate one man and break another.[52]

Mordecai ordered she conceal her Jewish identity (2:10), but now Esther commands[53] Mordecai and her people to "Go, gather . . . fast for me" (4:15–17). The exchange between these two characters (one female and one male via a

51. Mordecai saves Xerxes' life (ch. 2). When Jews are in danger, Xerxes turns his responsibility over to Mordecai (ch. 8). Either Xerxes' is indifferent or he trusts Mordecai to again save.

52. Fox, 66.

53. Qal imperative.

male messenger) at this pivotal moment creates a "delay" (three days) in the flow of events (4:16; 5:1), heightening the story's suspense before transitioning to Esther's meeting with Xerxes and Haman (again, one female with two male characters in conversation). Her character development, expressed in her resolve to appear before Xerxes, is made apparent through her firsthand engagement with a written document and in the pointed dialogue with a community member who deconstructs her interpretations. Without option for self-preservation, she resorts to unconventional means to gain Xerxes' attention (4:16).

Esther's interaction with Mordecai defines the challenge of violating court protocol (v. 11), with the threat of execution raising the stakes considerably. Mordecai's former actions, however, serve as a paradigm for Esther. Mordecai's refusal to bow to Haman (3:2) makes him conspicuous in a crowd where everyone does obeisance.[54] He "stands out" by donning unacceptable clothing (4:1–2) and positioning himself at the limits his garb will take him (4:2—"But he went only as far as the king's gate, because no one clothed in sackcloth was allowed to enter it"). His character portrayal and actions of self-abandonment serve as an example for Esther, who now, as a countercultural actress, will seek access to the king (5:1) in order to reveal her hidden identity (4:1; 7:3–6). She mirrors Mordecai's breach of etiquette (3:3) when committing to call on Persia's monarch (4:11), yet uses clothing to her advantage for access, rather than limitation. Mordecai's infraction (rending his clothes; sitting in sackcloth at the king's gate [vv. 1–2]) as well as Esther's unsolicited appearance before Xerxes, are each punishable acts (inferred in v. 2 and stated in v. 11), yet neither character is ever reprimanded nor put to death. Rather, their clandestine communication (ch. 4) anticipates public disclosure

54. Fox, 45.

(Chapter 7); Mordecai's rending his garments and refusing new wardrobe thus become a subtle stratagem for Esther's irrevocable unveiling of her identity (7:4).

Character in Action (Esther Chapters 5–8)

(Readers are encouraged to refer to the study questions for these chapters found in appendix 1.)

Esther's confrontation with a writing leads to her struggle with what the text means (for her and her people). Her deliberations with Mordecai lead the "weak" or "small" female queen to a point of personal resolve to call on the great male king. Esther's identification with Mordecai is a relationship representing a larger community bond. In the mix of events, the revelation of her identity exposes the story's villain and his conspiracy.

The Small Calls on the Great: The Royal Stage

Stylistic use of irony artistically crafts the circumstances for Esther's request of the king. The invitation for Xerxes and Haman to attend her feast (5:4) follows her "command" to Mordecai and her people to fast (4:16). In a realm of indulgence where men tell women what to do, a woman (Esther) issues an order for self-denial to a man.[55] In a story where men routinely sit and drink, but not with women (1:7–9), Esther crosses social custom by inviting men to her drinking party (5:4 and 7:1–2). Further, in an empire of excessiveness where possessions are emphatically the king's (Vashti in the *king's* house [1:9]), Xerxes' acceptance of Esther oddly includes his extreme pledge to her of (only) "half the kingdom" (5:6; 7:2)—a "gift" (or bribe) she refuses (like Mordecai's rejection of new garments). The limited or controlled perspective of Xerxes, who focuses on "half the

55. Qal imperative; 4:16.

kingdom," is contrasted to the wider vision of Esther, whose sights are set on saving Jews in "the whole kingdom."[56]

Curiously, Vashti disobeys a summons, forfeiting her place as queen (ch. 1). Esther's reply to Mordecai declares similar potential for censure and punishment (4:11), yet the events of the narrative are portrayed in a manner depicting triumph. Overcoming a kingdom's oppressiveness of disenfranchised people(s) is anticipated via subtle variance in the actions of both women: Vashti is to come, she did not appear before Xerxes, and she is banished (1:10–22); in contrast Esther is not to appear uninvited, she calls on Xerxes, but ultimate banishment (death) is never imposed (chs. 4–8). Esther is "queen in Vashti's place," and the crafting of her character mirrors Vashti's countercultural protest; she is all the more like her predecessor in crossing social lines. Esther's distinction, though, will be an achievement in contrast to how the former queen was limited. Where Vashti's protest is made with no record of her words (ch. 1), Esther's quoted speeches intercede for those who otherwise have no voice.

Esther's second invitation to Xerxes (5:6–8) reveals nervousness and humility, concurrently raising the plot's pitch through further delay. This postponement extends

56. Goldingay aptly and eloquently surveys the sense of irony in the narrative with other examples: "Ahaseurus deposes one assertive queen to replace her with another whose assertiveness has much more effect on imperial policy. Haman has to honor Moredecai in the way he would like to be honored, welcomes the invitation to a dinner at which he is robbed of the chance to execute his plan, throws himself on Esther's mercy and is thought to be trying to rape her, and finally hangs on the gallows he built for Mordecai. Mordecai takes over Haman's house and his position, and the king permits the Judahites to slaughter their enemies rather than being slaughtered. The casting of lots (Purim) that Haman intended should bring the Judahites' annihilation becomes the commemoration of their deliverance" (*Israel's Gospel*, 785).

in the scene honoring Mordecai (ch. 6), an episode where Esther again is clearly absent.

The Vital Role of Mordecai Revisited

Haman has "no satisfaction as long as" he sees "Mordecai sitting at the king's gate" (5:13). Mordecai's humility contrasts Haman's arrogance. The self-abasing Jew is exalted and his arrogant antagonist is dismally disgraced.

Xerxes hosts parties, endorses edicts, chooses a wife-queen, promotes a counselor, and drinks wine, but he cannot sleep (6:1). His Sominex material is reading the kingdom's record. Offsetting self-absorption with his realm, Xerxes learns Mordecai rescued his life (2:21–23), and under the cloak of darkness (night) recognizes no reward is recorded (6:3). Haman's unannounced visit (and undeclared intentions to seek Mordecai's execution [5:14; 6:4–5]) is not met with death, though his ego is assassinated when Xerxes, to reward Mordecai, uses Haman's advice against him ("do just as *you* have suggested for Mordecai the Jew" [6:10]).

Haman's frustrated attempts to seek Mordecai's death lead to personal shame. He ironically reverses his own prominence as his proposal is set into motion by a king who uses the vizier's words against him (v. 10). He decorates and parades Mordecai before a kingdom (v. 11), in contrast to a kingdom's parade before men (1:4). Mordecai's head is crowned to the empire's accolades (broad, great expanse) (6:11), whereas Haman's head is later covered and he returns home (small and local) (v. 12). At his residence, the locus of his rule as a man (1:22), he hears words of ruin declared in the voice of (note!) a woman, his wife, Zeresh (6:13). Her speech anticipates Esther's voice, who quotes Haman's pogrom for Jewish extermination as the very formula for Haman's demise (7:3–4). While Esther is not present in the events of chapter 6, this passage anticipates her public accomplishment of self-exposure and defeat of a foe (ch. 7).

This section of delay (ch. 6) offers readers pause to anticipate Esther's future role in the example of Mordecai.

Esther—A Leader Unlike Haman

Competing for obtuseness,[57] Haman assumes flattery from the king, but is ironically humiliated by his own words (6:12). He assumes honor banqueting with Xerxes ("I'm the only person" [5:12]), but is exposed as a vile rebel. Xerxes uses Haman's speech to honor Mordecai—"do just as you have suggested" (6:10)—and Esther quotes Haman's words (destruction, slaughter, annihilation) to reveal his conspiracy (3:13; 7:4). The narrative may paint Esther in the varied character traits of Vashti and Mordecai, but she is clearly not at all like Haman—a contrast accented in at least four key ways: in a theme of "rising and falling," in the story's use of clothing, in acts of sitting and drinking, and in a controversial use of corporal punishment.

Rising and Falling

Haman desires Mordecai bow (3:2), but satirically "falls" in "grief" before the Jew (6:11–12). The once exalted male leader who toyed with the lives of others (3:1, 8–9) falls before Queen Esther pleading for his own existence (7:7–8). He finally and paradoxically falls through ultimate elevation on seventy five foot gallows he himself had ordered built (5:14; 7:9–10).

His schemes pursued "Mordecai who would not move," plotting the Jew "will be moved" and "hanged from a gallows in order to make him permanently immobile."[58] Xerxes executed two malefactors,[59] yet Haman's penchant

57. Van Wijk-Bos, 100.

58. Ibid., 93.

59. On "gallows"(2:23); the KJV renders עץ [*ets*] as "tree," though עץ in 5:14, 6:4, 7:9, and 8:7 is rendered "gallows."

to outdo others is evinced in his requirement for bigger and specifically measured forms of execution. Odd as it is, just how high do gallows have to be in order to carry out a death sentence? The specified height of Haman's gallows functions to contrast the lack of dimension given for the king's gallows. The stylistic disparity suggests Haman's attempt to exalt himself, even above Xerxes; an incipient aspect of his proposal of honor in chapter 6. Sarcasm further adds insult to injury in that Haman's order for gallows of this measure is not a self-devised idea. His actions are responsive to Zeresh, his wife (*woman*) and friends (5:14), oddly "reminding us of the ironic but inevitable thwarting of the king's decree that every *man* [emphasis mine] shall rule his own house (1:22)."[60]

In contrast to death threats, Esther characteristically stands for life. She reports (2:22) an assassination attempt on Xerxes' life—a communication advancing Mordecai and shaming Haman (6:10–13). Her next report of a "death" threat (chs. 7–8) brings final "elevation" for both Haman and Mordecai, in Haman's decisive shaming (execution by elevation on his own seventy-five-foot means of death) and Mordecai's definitive advancement and promotion in the kingdom's administration (8:2). The narrative qualities play out in role reversal where Haman and Mordecai "trade places"; at the king's command, Haman takes the place of death intended for Mordecai, whereas Mordecai takes Haman's office by royal act. In each episode (ch. 2 and chs. 7–8), Esther is the selfless agent of communication emerging as an intercessor and deliverer who acts for the preservation of life. Defending people comes to, and stems from, her wrestling with implications of a text (4:14). She is, thus, contrasted to the subversive, furtive, conniving Haman, who writes and acts for selfishly motivated forms of oppression, threat, and death. Esther's contrast to Haman's character is

60. Fox, 74.

further apparent in her use of clothing and in the acts of sitting and drinking.

Clothing and Shaping Personae

The story's use of clothing is a revealing example of literary artistry! Garments are conspicuous emblems of rank; they are costumes of power, signaling class, and move the theme of "reversal" along. The empire's décor brandishes blue (or violet) and white hangings (1:6), and Mordecai's later robes of honor are of similar hue (8:15) (also, "gold"). These colors correspond with an empire enamored by masculine power.[61] Identifying with the king (power) features prominently in a contest between Agagite and Jew; Haman postures for "a royal robe the king has worn" (6:8).[62] To Haman's chagrin, Mordecai receives the patent status symbols his nemesis coveted (6:10–11). In the shaping of personae, Mordecai receives that which he never desired; Haman loses what he lusted after (and more).

Esther "put on" her royal robes (5:1)—an act matching her royal stature.[63] Her first visit to Xerxes says nothing of clothes (2:15–17), but 5:1 clearly stages her new attitude in life.[64] Omitting details about clothing (2:15–18) binds Esther to Vashti (who is to appear with her crown as the one mandatory accessory [1:11]). Esther's robing (5:1) is of her own volition, and she determines to meet Xerxes though she has not been called.

The theme of reversal is even sublimated in granting and withholding crowns: Vashti has a crown (1:11), and

61. R. Pfeiffer, 478; Keil and Delitzsch, 325.

62. For Berlin, Haman's desire for the king's robe and horse "is not a casual suggestion. It means that Haman wants to masquerade as the king" ("Esther and Ancient Storytelling," 11).

63. Craig, 95.

64. Ibid.

Esther has a "royal" crown (2:17); Mordecai wears a large golden crown (8:15), and Haman covets, but is denied Xerxes' crown (6:6–10).[65] Haman's head, rather, is cloaked in shame (6:12; 7:8), and when Xerxes perceives Haman (with no crown) "attacks" the queen (who is with crown) (7:8), the king interprets Haman's act as rebellion. The breach of etiquette is met with an immediate order to "hang him" (v. 9), changing the status of his head. As Haman was swiftly promoted by the king (ch. 3), he is quickly whisked away for execution ("elevation" on the seventy-five-foot gallows). Rather than cover his own head and depart, unnamed attendants cloak Haman's head (7:8),[66] and escort him to his death.

Sitting and Drinking

Haman desires complete eradication of the Jews (3:12–13) only to learn Esther's life is part of the mix (7:3–4). Xerxes enjoys wine and beautiful women, both of which Esther uses to unmask Haman's conspiracy. Her testimony ends Haman's administration of terror, shaping her as an effective, proactive counteragent to unethical, politically charged ethnic discrimination and behavior.

In this story, men exercise choice in the liberality of drink, and women are not specifically mentioned as present when males imbibe (1:6–8; recast in 3:15). Contrasting how chapter 1 exalts males and segregates females, Esther crosses cultural norms when inviting men to drink with her.

65. The NIV renders 6:8 as a "royal crest" for the horse, rather than a bit more ambiguous reference to (his or its) "crown royal" in the KJV that either servant or stallion could wear. Berlin comments, "Modern exegetes understand that the crown was on the horse's head, but earlier exegetes interpreted the phrase to mean the crown was on the king's head, as reflected in the KJV" ("Esther and Ancient Storytelling," 13).

66. Van Wijk-Bos, 103.

The narrative uses wine and women to paint oppression and demoralization as part and parcel of the kingdom; but in an empire where men sit and drink, Esther now reclines at a wine feast with men present (7:8).[67] This scene obviates three actions for brief consideration: Esther's quotes of Haman posit her as an information-bearer; Haman's act of "falling" on the couch before the queen; and the interpretive issue of the queen's posture "sitting" on the couch where Haman "falls."

Esther as Information-Bearer

Esther emerges as an information-bearer (7:3–6); this is an act men primarily do in this story. In contrast to Haman who had conveniently left off the detail of his victim's national identity (ch. 3), Esther's specificity in quoting Haman unmasks his treachery, forcing Xerxes to choose between vizier and queen. Xerxes leaves the wine feast and deliberates in the garden (7:7), a detail emphasizing Xerxes' separation from Haman (whom he drinks with on other occasions [3:15]). Commensurate with Haman's speedy promotion (3:1–2), Xerxes rapidly judges him (7:8–10). The superb crafting of this episode mimics the actions of a prior scene where a woman (Vashti) does not leave with an escort to meet a king who would not leave his wine and she is "eliminated" (1:19); now a king leaves his wine and

67. R. Pfeiffer observes drinking episodes honor the text's segregation of gender, though he cites Neh 2:6 and Dan 5:2 as examples where men and women occasionally drink together in the Persian world (478). In Neh 2:1–6, however, the queen sat and only the king drinks. Dan 5:2 may be a generalization, as the locality of women in the story is not spelled out; the narrator specifies the queen had come into the banquet house to make her announcement (v. 10). While hardly a point to lock swords over, segregation in the story of Esther injects the conflict with added gravity.

subsequently sentences a man who is accompanied to his own gallows for death (7:6–10).

Haman's Act of "Falling" on the Couch

Xerxes' analysis of Haman "bowing" (falling) on Esther's couch (7:8) cynically insults Haman as "an aggressor against his queen-wife." Haman never gains Xerxes' complete confidence; rather, Haman is repeatedly cast as the frustrated brunt of his king's assessments: 7:8 is set against a background where Haman cannot fully bribe the king (3:11); Xerxes respects Mordecai at Haman's expense (6:12); and the king delights in Esther protecting her life, but does not spare Haman (7:5, 9–10).

The king's scrutiny of Haman's "falling" on the couch is fraught with more import than initially meets the eye; this act is not dismissed by the king as a passing misunderstanding. Haman is accused of plotting against Esther (though this was unknown to him), and his actions are (*mis*)interpreted by the king as the vizier's intent to molest the queen. This perception is taken as a personal affront to the king, predicated on Esther's quote of Haman's speech (the initial trigger of the king's angry reaction and momentary departure to the garden). The quotes of Haman show his own words have a way of tripping him. The king used Haman's very words to honor Mordecai (ch. 6), unwittingly shaming Haman. He now condemns himself in his own words and deeds (ch. 7), followed by his dying (falling) on his own gallows (v. 10).[68]

Beyond the scope of entertaining interpretive possibilities informed by retribution theology (sow-reap ideas), the story paints an example sufficient enough to caution the

68. "Enemies can sometimes be thwarted by letting them have their way, and that victory can come disguised as defeat" (Copenhaver, "Conspiracy of Deliverance," 811). See also, Josephus: *Antiquities* 11.6.1–13.

use of words and deeds contrary to life or benefit to others: "In the long run the tyrant is weaker than is his victims."[69]

Esther's "Sitting" on the Couch

Haman is ironically executed for a crime he did not commit—in the king's eyes Haman is guilty of attempted rape.[70] A case for Esther's "deception"[71] in Haman's "guilt" is tenuous at best: the idea she sits provocatively is speculative; 7:8 only says she reclines, not "how" she is sitting. Significantly, this is the sole account in the narrative of a woman "sitting," and that at wine. Thus, a dramatic shift occurs as Esther, a symbol of countercultural action, like Vashti, challenges gender assumptions of power, bravely crossing societal boundaries and sitting in the company of drinking men.

> Vashti's refusal to be an object of display is in a real sense a refusal to be objectivized, hence, to be robbed of her subjectivity. Esther's insistence on appearing, albeit using the tools of display (5:1: "On the third day, Esther put on her royal robes"), is the positive version of Vashti's negative act; she appears not for show but for action, not as sheer possession but as a self-possessed subject, and to drive this continuity between Esther and Vashti home, it is now *she* who makes the king appear at *her* banquet.[72]

69. Guthmann, "Passover," 122.

70. Goldman, 19. Berlin comments, "Ahaseurus has identified the right crime (treason) for the wrong reason. As is fitting for a comic farce, the villain gets the punishment he deserves for something he did not do" ("Esther and Ancient Storytelling," 14).

71. Fuchs, "For I Have the Way of Women," 70.

72. Bal, "Lots of Writing," 92–93.

Haman inadvertently conspired against Esther. She refutes and reverses his plan,[73] in the use of his own words, followed by the king misinterpreting Haman's actions. Overturning court custom and crossing lines of gender expectation makes Esther a pivotal figure in the rise and fall of key leaders of this story, illustrating how the plot "is a series of events . . . a selection and organization of events in a particular order of time; it is a purposeful structure built around the conflict between the personae."[74]

Courageous Queen or Cruel Conspirator?

A fourth feature of Esther's distance from Haman is her call for the public display of Haman's deceased sons. Themes of revenge and retribution are scrutinized in scholarly work, accusing Esther as a "cruel queen."[75] The indictment stems from an ethical dilemma posed by Esther's silence at Haman's sentencing, and more so her treatment of his ten dead sons (Esther's conduct toward Zeresh, Haman's wife, is left unstated) (9:10, 14).[76] These concerns have led to assuming the book is too nationalistic. However, factors of the narrative have readied readers for this episode, requiring exploration of how antecedent scenes function in the story at large. Subjective verdicts on Esther's actions must consider at least three aspects of the narrative: Esther is cast as an actress for justice in this story; the storyteller's penchant for

73. Goldman, 22.

74. Amit, 47.

75. See, for example, comments reviewed in R. Pfeiffer, 482; and Fox, 115.

76. Readers are left to speculate on Zeresh's status: is she "banished" or does she become a house-slave when Xerxes gives Haman's house to Esther (8:1–3) who subsequently transfers the estate to Mordecai (8:3)? This does not appear to be of central concern for the narrator. Zeresh's role is concise; like Vashti, she makes a brief appearance, makes her point, and makes an exit.

pointing out excess or exaggeration; and the narrator's style of emphasizing reversals. With death as a note of finality (anticipated in Haman's plot against Mordecai), the reversal of the plot results in the death of Haman and his sons; the "contest" focuses more on life, answering in this scene the question of "Who will endure?"

Esther's order to publicly display corpses is an odd command for a "second death" (9:6–10, 13–14). The nature of retaliation leads to pejorative readings of the queen's actions,[77] yet, to limit this concern solely to retribution at her hands ignores Haman had initiated the attack on the Jewish people (3:13). Esther is not elsewhere cast as an aggressor; rather, she consistently seeks justice for, and acts in defense of, others (she relayed information about an assassination threat on the king's life [ch. 2]; she sends clothing to Mordecai, likely to bypass the possibility of his death [ch. 4]; and she risks her own life on behalf of her people [ch. 4]). As a queen who seeks life and not death in this story, it is unfair to dismiss her as now surfacing some dark side. It must be noted Haman's ten sons are already dead when Esther requests their hanging (9:6–10, 13–14); this is a bit more humane than demanding torture and death and may function as contemporary news reports: there is no masking of hard realities. Those responsible for the conflict have come to an end—"See for yourself: Haman and his clan are gone." While difficult and fraught with problems, Esther's action is at least an exposure of truth (showing the dead sons), contrasting the deception of Haman (ch. 3) to exterminate the living whose identity was (conveniently) kept from Xerxes.

In chapter 2, young virgins are gathered and exploited by a selfish king. Levenson suggests the book makes its points through indirection, allowing one to infer that life

77. Levenson, "Scroll of Esther," 442.

for the virgins has come to an end (or is at least, redefined by subjugation). Once gathered, one is left to wonder what happens to these nameless, faceless girls (v. 11). By contrast, Esther is forthcoming and leaves no room for speculation. In a story of reversals, it is now the end of Haman's male progeny that is publicly displayed; they (male Agagites) perish while she (female Jewess), along with her people (the Jews), will live. The public display of the deceased functions as a symbol of which people endures. Hanging on a tree is a sign of cursing and makes appeal to practices and theology of Deuteronomy (a feature possibly important to the early Jewish community of readers or to the narrator who emphasizes this point). The idea is proverbial; the one who laid the snare was caught in his own trap. At the very least, by acting in self-defense, the character of Esther as an agent of life is distanced further from the character of Haman the oppressor. For Haman, publicly displaying a living Mordecai on gallows until he is dead was a selfish goal. The queen rather calls for the public display of already dead oppressors, demonstrating tyranny has ended and Jews are now free.

The difficulties of the passage show the cultural baggage readers bring to the text as a lens of critique is shaped on the basis of contemporary ethics. The direction of this inquiry takes readers into interpretive areas beyond the scope of this particular study. Speculation offers this is a comic act adding insult to injury,[78] where "judgment" is inflicted on oppressors and the association of a family with Haman is judged on the very instrument of death he built for exterminating the family (nation) of Jews (5:14). The

78. For Craig, the "second death" scene is comic rather than real, functioning didactically without the death of real people. As "applied wisdom" (Talmon, 427), the text is a moral teaching from ancient Israel personifying attributes of good and evil in characters of a story (Levenson, "Scroll of Esther," 443).

story advances the idea of victory; there will be no more sons to propagate the line of the Amalekite oppressor (Exod 17). Esther epitomizes the end of a conflict; not only in her story world, but in the larger confines of the Jewish struggle. If the Saul-Agag drama does indeed shadow the story of Esther, the predicate account of Exodus 17 finds fulfillment in this exilic story; the promise of ongoing strife with Amalek (and his seed) now ends. The public display of ten already dead "sons" typifies not just the concept of ending male oppression, but also the idea that Haman's family line and terror has ended. The Jews will endure; their oppressors will not.

The ethics of such a decision remain difficult and challenging. Perhaps the sense of liberty formed in the passage asks consideration of the thought: "Man must destroy war, or war will destroy man."[79] Of equal import is Goldingay's conclusion where humor intertwines in how this might read the readers: "Perhaps the story invites laughing Judahites to see themselves as just as bad as their persecutors if they behave in the same way when they have the opportunity."[80] The narrative offers some corrective by a narrator's tack that differentiates aggression by enemies and acts of self-defense by Jews. Admittedly, the case at large remains open and laden with ethical baggage.

Character in Solidarity (Esther Chapters 9–10)

(Readers are encouraged to refer to the study questions for these chapters found in appendix 1.)

79. Guthman, 123. "Man" is here understood as inclusive of humankind. Goldman also observes the function here of the massacre as not "real" but a challenge of conscience through the reader's exposure to ethical ironies (25).

80. Goldingay, *Israel's Gospel*, 786.

Esther's select pronouns ("my people"; "I and my people"; "we" [7:3–4]) publicly assert her once-silent ancestry (2:5–7). She moves "beyond the familiarity and safety of court life in support of a moral cause,"[81] celebrating the deconstruction of hegemonious powers. In terms of feasts, Persian revelry (1:7–8) contrasts Jewish Purim (9:18); the first toasts "wealth and power," the latter honors "deliverance and survival."[82]

The story's oppressors are males who sit, sip wine, settle on people's fate, and send death threats; the crisis concludes with a female who forgoes food and drink (4:16) framing and dispatching a letter. Contrasting Haman who feasts and sends death threats to Jews (ch. 3), Esther fasts (4:16) and writes to her people about joyous feasting and giving food-gifts to the less fortunate (9:29–30). Xerxes celebrates "release" and gift-giving on account of Esther (2:18); in chapter 9, she is again an agent of transformation in a kingdom of marginalization where people now are released from death and send gifts. She stands with her people under threat of death and celebrates with them in life. Thus, "Esther herself, who was cut off from her people, provides an example of liberation through solidarity with the victims of oppression."[83]

The Small Celebrate Great Deconstruction: A New Stage

Through satire and turnabout, gender and social conflicts force the tension of freedom versus oppression to the forefront. The countercultural refusal to be *man*-aged by the structure-legitimating forces of a male-dominated society forms a cohesive story line beginning with the silent Vashti

81. Rosenblatt, "Portraits of Heroism," 49.

82. Levenson, *Esther*, 44.

83. Van Wijk-Bos, 67.

(to whom the narrator creatively gives no voice). The story develops its critique through: (1) a male power figure (king) who cannot make decisions alone and a vast kingdom over which he "rules"; (2) the personal contest for superiority between a self-seeking "noble" and a selfless Jew; and (3) most significantly a young, beautiful Jewish woman who is queen "in Vashti's stead" (see 2:4).[84]

Esther succeeds where Vashti is hindered as she triumphantly critiques the kingdom. The personal success of Mordecai and Esther embody the essential corporate concerns of the Jewish people. Their local victories become the shared success of the Jewish nation at large (9:18–22). Issuing the initial two edicts is to rid the realm of Vashti and the Jews (1:19; 3:13), but Mordecai and Esther send decrees to defend their people (who survive crisis) (8:9–10). The story also advances the point that antagonists like Memucan and Haman get more than they bargain for. It is in the end, after all, a virtuous woman who achieves a countercultural victory!

The story begins with revelry and ends in festivity. It reflects on the "victimized" as "vindicated" (9:19). Jews celebrate freedom (chs. 9–10), contrasting the empire's gala control of property and people (ch. 1). The subjugated of 1:9 were reserved in the limits of a house, as those "free" made merry outdoors. Territorial descriptions amplify Xerxes' realm (ch. 1), but the book ends with Jews of the empire feasting (9:18–19); and Xerxes stays in "his" headquarters, "*distant*" from people (10:1). He taxes his kingdom and a parting comment summarizes (satirizes) his "acts of power" (v. 2). In contrast, Mordecai's commitment to care for people (2:7; 10:3) receives greater literary space and emphasis, poking a final jab at the conflict between life choices. Critiqued are the attitudes of "taking (taxing) and control" (victimiza-

84. "While the Hebrew version is framed by powerful men, it is dominated by audacious women" (Goldingay, *Israel's Gospel*, 780).

tion), versus "giving and selfless concern" for the welfare of others (vindication).[85] Thus, the Esther story stands "as a symbol of hope in the face of persecution."[86]

The Vital Role of Esther: Where Is She?

The epilogue (10:1–3) contrasts two named men: Xerxes and Mordecai; yet, as in chapters 3 and 6, Esther is neither named nor present![87] Amit observes:

> While events are dynamic, the opening is descriptive, meaning . . . it is static, while the ending marks the exit of personae and returns the reader to the static condition of the opening. Nevertheless, in a story with a concentric ending, the hero or heroes only seem to return to the condition from which they had set out, because the events have affected them—and the reader with them. The reality to which they return is not the same as it was.[88]

85. Taxation versus plundering (Levenson, *Esther*, 132). If 2:18 means Xerxes suspended taxes, it is ironic he fronts an exorbitant amount for Haman (3:9–11) and is willing to give 50 percent of his kingdom to Esther (5:6; 7:2). The Talmud ponders he gave gifts and repealed taxes (ch. 2) to woo disclosure of her national origin (XVIII. N.1), but the story itself does not reveal his motives.

86. Laffey's review of Craig's "Reading Esther," 342.

87. Readers are reminded of the English translations used most often in study. This observation does not ignore the potentially chiastic structure of the book, which begins and ends with men of the kingdom. Rather, as the celebration of Purim includes the tasty delicacies of delightful foods, what is that last flavor of the book readers take with them? Possibly due to the imposed chapter and verse designations of our English texts, readers more likely depart with a final note of Mordecai's victory and the king's quiet receding into the sunset, without questioning, "Where is Esther?!"

88. Amit, 36. Reorientation results: see Brueggemann's *Message of the Psalms* (orientation, disorientation, reorientation), and Brown's *Character in Crisis* on the Wisdom Literature (character formed,

The intentionality of artistic construction here bespeaks the pleasing nature of literary art in this biblical text to craft a specific point; thus, "artists must necessarily be concerned as much with the details of a work as with the overall effect."[89] The effect in this story is necessarily the noted absence of Esther.

The story starts with Xerxes and his men drinking liberally in a lavish garden, indicative of the near proximity of a male king and his male court (1:4–8). Women are segregated indoors and the narrator remarks the space belongs to the male king (v. 9), who in effect has so distanced himself from that which is apparently inferior in his eyes. Vashti, after all, had to be called for and was to be escorted from another location to the king's presence. The epilogue (10:1), though, now casts the king as a *distant* monarch. While power shifts (now the oppressed freely celebrate), it is not readily apparent if the Persian system is greatly altered.

The static condition of chapter 1 paints a scene of relative female absence, and chapter 10, telescoping from a literary context connected with chapter 9, returns to this status quo.[90] However, life is not the same for Xerxes; he is king, but now *he* (not the women of 1:9) is insulated by a narrator's comment. Life is not the same for Mordecai; he is no longer oppressed.[91] Life is not the same for Esther. She

---

deformed, and reformed). While the genre of poetic literature differs from the review of narrative in this project, helpful thought is yielded in these works.

89. Sasson, in Wenham's "Coherence of the Flood Narrative," 340.

90. The text's symmetry may well be in view here. The chiastic structure of the book is taken up in Levenson's commentary. I contend the structure raises the question: "If readers were paying attention to the narrative's details in the opening scene, does that scene of relative female absence again challenge us as the text concludes?"

91. Craig critiques views where Mordecai masterminds Esther's

advances herself, the plight of women, and her people, the, Jews in unprecedented fashion. Her character and actions demonstrate she "is a sage, not a sex-object."[92] Yet, the final chapter could seem almost hollow without her presence, begging again the question: "Where is Esther?"

Esther—Like Us or Not Like Us

Thus, "is there really a change for us as readers?" Indeed hidden, yet, in plain sight throughout the narrative, these final verses require a look for Esther, leaving readers "to decide how to evaluate this story in light of their own contexts and concerns."[93] Xerxes may be a powerful king, but the story paints him more as a mere jester in royal robes. While change occurs, "the fool or clown is the king of this upside-down world,"[94] and Esther, the character of obscurity, rules. Thus, the odd ending "silently" tests our moral judgment as readers,[95] determining if we learn anything at all about the treatment of people (and reading methods) among us who (that) are incorrectly and inappropriately deemed weak.

Summary

This reading offers one literary analysis of select English translations of the MT Esther; it is not the final word on this text. This reading avoids historical-critical issues dem-

actions; she devised the plan to outwit Haman by herself. Jones concurs (176). Talmon adds, "In the course of events she ascends from the role of Mordecai's protégé to become her mentor's guardian. In fact she completely overshadows her uncle and outclasses his adversary Haman in the art of crafty planning and successful execution. In the end it is Esther's superior cleverness which saves the day" (449).

92. Jones, 177.

93. Humphreys, 340.

94. Craig, 138.

95. Goldman, 26.

onstrating how biblical studies methods can potentially and directly engage a story world as an initial entry into exploration of that story world itself. While historical-critical features are not devalued, questions of authorship, audience, date of composition, and place of writing are not thoroughly investigated in this reading. There is no significant attempt to reconstruct the community behind the text. Rather, the narrative is read on the basis of its own story world, and from that arena, implications regarding the literature, social interests, and theology, whether apparent or implied, can be studied further.

Character formation is explored by examining how the narrative creates space for Esther's entrance into the story world, her direct or implied association with other characters, and the crisis she faces. Esther's words and deeds (commands, donning clothes, calling on the king) cast her as an emerging agent of transition as she moves from relative obscurity to prominence. Her interaction with key male actors posits her as the pivotal figure leading to the exalting or debasing of other characters.

This reading is sensitive to the components of biblical narrative, expressed as a collection of observations. These observations are declared, discussed, and documented, and relationships between those observations are entertained. In the next section, pedagogical elements from this reading are distilled, moving toward a model for reading biblical narrative.

3

Findings

"Theology should come from the Bible itself, not the system I bring to the Scriptures."

—Paul R. House[1]

IMPLICATIONS FROM this reading for studying biblical story include, but are not limited to: acknowledging the integrated features of biblical narrative; identification of presuppositions and nuances that shape a lens of reading; and an appreciation of literary art that intersects a reader's humanity with the humanity of characters presented in the story. The narrative (and its structure) confronts the reader (and her/his personal disposition as a reader) in community with other readers, to delineate outcomes geared toward the transmission of meaning and call to action.

Appreciation for literary art results by acknowledging the integrated features of biblical narrative. The creation of space in the opening scenes shapes an empire of marginalization in the numeric repetition of provinces, rehearsing the vast boundaries of the kingdom, and an all-male drinking party. The room given to masculine revelry contrasts a single verse of female celebration. This is Esther's stage as an alien on two fronts: she is a female and a national Jew(ess). She faces oppression in foreign territory due to

1. House, *Old Testament Theology*, 7.

gender and ethnicity, yet uses the empire's tools of wine and women against itself. Her character development parallels Mordecai's acts; he rends his garments to prepare for the unveiling of her character to the king.

Admitted nuances shaping a lens of reading recognize the Esther story as a unique piece of literature, yet a story informed by, and connected with, Israel's narrative history. Affinities with the Joseph story (Gen 37–50), for example, posit a Jewish descendent who finds approval in a foreign monarch's court and antagonists who stage their opposition to an innocent victim in scenes of eating and drinking. Other scenes are equally the platform for transposition as in the Daniel stories (i.e., Dan 5; an inept foreign monarch throws a lavish drinking party; a woman's voice deconstructs male excesses; and an innocent Jew finds favor). What one brings to the text of reading is impacted by their familiarity with other biblical narratives.

Underdogs are cheered; rogues are jeered. Readers identify with Esther and Mordecai as they salute the heroes and hate the villain. The crafting of narrative art in the Esther story recognizes how human action and speech, shared by readers and the narrative's characters, are an interface to the story world. Esther's gender and ethnic challenges, in an arena of oppression, are elements of life's struggles held in common by readers and story characters. The Esther story holds out hope for readers living in exile; readers who look for models to emulate in their own struggles and crises.

This reading of Esther demonstrates how literary-critical studies augment existing reading methods and inform a potential research paradigm. I will briefly discuss each of these and propose four primary components for a reading method that emerge from the Esther story (what comes to a text; reading the text; seeking meaning from a text, and application of what is learned from a text). This section will conclude with a general summary of how this method critiques current reading practices.

Augmenting Methods

This project does not "banish" nor advocate "erasure"[2] of existing reading techniques. To do so would only parallel Haman's attitude of extinguishing others. Equally of import, this project does not intentionally seek to ignore the value and contribution of other reading methods; such ignorance would follow Xerxes' inept and selfish leadership. Rather, this project demonstrates how literary-critical studies, following Esther's example, supplement existing research practices in various ministry contexts[3] by reading the literature on its own merits.

A literary-critical reading of Esther differs from, but compliments historical-critical interests. For example, this reading does not name an author behind the text; it avoids arguing which historical Persian monarch is represented; or if Mordecai is identified with *Marduka* (a contemporary of this exilic period).[4] This reading stresses, however, observations on a select book and literary genre, where relationship of story features to events, characters, actions, and speeches form consistent themes and compare characters for critique (Esther to Vashti and Mordecai; Mordecai and Esther to Haman).

Literary-critical readings in some ministry contexts are (in effect) in exile and marginalized in deference to other interests, spending more time on a biblical book's background rather than teaching students reading methods and empowering them to discover the biblical story world themselves. Practices that ignore reading what the text itself says (and

2. See Beal.

3. See Osborne, *The Hermeneutical Spiral*, 164–68 on "weaknesses" of narrative criticism.

4. See Clines, "Quest for the Historical Mordecai," 129–36.

how the text says it) lead students toward an agenda of what "they should believe," rather than teaching them how to discover a message(s) they can embrace as their own. The imbalance inadvertently silences the value and need for supplemental reading methods. Introducing skills in reading biblical narrative cannot be polarized to assume conditional acceptance means validation as another trophy of hermeneutical control. Implementing literary-critical skills in Christian education contexts must not wait for permission from other critical camps to move from periphery to center. Insulation in an illusion of safety, defined on the terms of dominant study practices, may cast a death sentence for other reading methods. A proactive resolve requires courses in literary-critical study follow Esther's example and don the beauty of what they have to offer (5:1), confront reading practices of neglect (even if risky), and stand with other hermeneutical options as valued complements to reading biblical texts.

Esther: Informing a Reading Methodology

Esther is the beautiful and humble queen a kingdom falls in love with (ch. 2). Though the masculine power base of the empire believes it has control, the sagely queen captures Xerxes' heart and the king validates her. Whether crossing court custom (4:11; 5:1–3) or when Haman is surprised he unknowingly included her in the death edict (7:6), her role is bound up in the confrontational nature of the silent Vashti, and (like her predecessor) Esther refuses to let persecution run rampant in a kingdom of oppression. This argues for learning to read biblical narrative in contexts of Christian education directly and confrontationally (like Vashti), as well as humbly (like Esther) where the beauty of such readings captivates readers (like Xerxes and his kingdom).

Without undue allegorizing of the story's actors, preferring favored hermeneutical postures may attempt to outdo or eliminate (as Haman) other valid readings; however, elitist practices work against themselves to their own demise. In contrast, affirming varied, valid reading approaches seeks life in place of stagnation and death (as Esther) (2:21–23; 7:3–4). Direct engagement with the text is a means for the common humanity of readers who speak, act, and write to interface a narrative world whose narrator speaks, acts, and writes in the telling of a story—a story where characters are shaped in their speeches, actions, and efforts at writing (edicts).

Proposing Parameters for a Reading Method

Christian education ministries (Bible Study groups, Sunday school classes, college-level courses, etc.) can follow Esther's model by presenting a queen who obliquely critiques, but does not dethrone her king.[5] Learning to read biblical narrative empowers teachers and students to acknowledge and name neglected hermeneutical practices in the curricular commitments of spiritual formation efforts, courses, and programs. Though this reading practice is available, its '"not having been called" (see 4:11) regularly leaves it currently hiding in plain sight before readers. This reading practice, however, is an agent of positive transformation (like Esther) as it serves to supplement other reading methods.

From the story of Esther, four major components inform a pedagogical construct in the act of reading biblical narrative: (1) The story world introduces Esther's back-

5. Literary-critical readings and historical-critical research together have a place in the hermeneutical quest of the biblical studies student. House remarks, "The ability to link text and history not only expands interpreters' knowledge of biblical backgrounds but also shows how theology was hammered out in the midst of everyday life and earth-shattering events" (71).

ground and the circumstances of her world; this information impacts her gender, ethnic, and political identity (chs. 1–2). *This is what she brings to the text* (chs. 3–4); (2) An edict requires she hermeneutically *engage a written text* (4:8); (3) In the quest for meaning, *she wrestles with implications* of the edict; in a community context, dialogue deconstructs her possible responses, ushering her to a (liminal) moment of decision; and (4) The crisis tests her *commitment* (chs. 7–8). She finds solidarity with those of a common lineage and experience, finally rejoicing in the community's perpetual celebration of Purim.

Esther's heritage and experience(s), text reading, struggle with implications of a document, and her commitment to live in community integrate as a model for Christian education; her liberation is their liberation, forming a paradigm for liberating readers. Pedagogically, a model for reading biblical narrative integrates at least these four major components and works toward:

(1) *Recognizing what readers bring to a text.* Esther's background, experience, gender, political rank, ethnicity, family ties, and the like, are factors in her personality coming to her reading of a text (4:8). This example prompts readers of biblical narratives to explore and identify what they bring (identity and experiences) to readings of a text. Where (and even how) readers are informed (or not) impacts the potential to read in a quality manner that honors the text itself; in sum, sensitivity to what is known, what lacks, individual strengths, and personal limitations collectively contribute to how subjective readings are helped or hindered.

(2) *A faithful searching of the Scriptures.* Esther engages the edict personally and directly. In a story where men tell women what to do, Mordecai, rather, sends a primary document for analysis. Esther understands the edict (v. 8) and her "reading" accompanies dialogue with the community

member, Mordecai (who weeps and wails over the news he himself has read). Contemporary readers of biblical narrative must not be content to be told what a story says through secondhand sources or merely accept the reports from other observers. Rather, personal, inductive, passionate engagement with primary sources and intentional community dialogue shape the potential for better understanding of texts and their implications.

(3) *A quest for meaning*. Esther learns of the edict by first hearing of Mordecai's distress (vv. 4–5) and repeated rounds of dialogue ensue (vv. 4–5; vv. 6–9: vv. 10–12; vv. 13–14; vv. 15–16). Her initial reaction is to "fix" the situation by clothing Mordecai in an insulated idealism (v. 4). Mordecai, however, deconstructs her interpretation of events (v. 4), returning a copy of the letter to the queen (v. 8); he clearly explains the edict, what it means, and lays the groundwork for her to explore potential avenues of action. He preempts her pondering to remain silent (vv. 13–14), leaving her accountable to the text and its implications. From this part of the story, contemporary readers are provided an example of challenges stemming from ignoring or reading "into" a text, as well as a role the community plays in the interpretive process. Further, all readings are not merely validated by the fact that they are read. The text remains the unalterable point of reference and the implications of the text cannot be ignored. Favoritism or personal penchant amounts to little more than sticking one's head in the sand. Propping up illusions may satisfy temporarily, but such practices do not invalidate the text nor do they honor it. Mordecai's deconstruction of Esther's musings forces her to ultimately deal with the reality of the text's implications. This quest for meaning holds truth above personal preference and calls the community to accountability.

(4) *A commitment to apply learned values in faithful confession to the world.* Esther resolves to go to Xerxes (vv. 8, 15–17). She lives in the light of what she learns the text means. Her personal and direct engagement with the letter and her involvement in community dialogue leads to resolution for action. Through self-denial (fasting) and self-sacrifice ("if I perish"), she aligns herself with those who need her. Her actions reinforce the integration of what readers bring to a text, readings of a text, and community dialogue. This integration prompts a response geared toward living faithfully in community with others.

Dr. Jackie Johns and Dr. Cheryl Bridges-Johns framed a four-movement model for the study of Scripture.[6] Their article, "Yielding to the Spirit," was released in the *Journal of Pentecostal Theology*, 1991. With a key feature of knowing God, emphasized in the Hebrew term, *yada* ("to know") (see also Thomas Groome's work),[7] they adeptly clarify the first movement of "Sharing Testimony" as a precursor to three following movements: Searching the Scriptures, Yielding to

6. See Johns and Bridges-Johns, "Yielding to the Spirit." To illustrate the model more definitively, a comparison of some contemporary works appear in the chart section.

A faith community's presence is assumed, offered by Johns and Bridges-Johns as "Sharing Testimony." In the Talmud of Babylonia, this feature is preserved by requiring the reading of Esther's story in an assembly of at least ten people (Neusner, *The Talmud of Babylonia*, 762, comment note on I.H.3). Also, Segovia's "sequence of instruction" has some overlap (*Decolonizing Biblical Studies*, 77).

Chart B page 145 can of course, be expanded by inclusion of other like-minded titles. The advantage of the model proposed by Johns and Bridges-Johns is the inclusion of the first element: what a reader brings to the text. The overarching advantage of the reading method proposed in this project is that the method itself emerges from the design and content of the biblical text itself. See examples in Briggs' work as well (*Reading the Bible Wisely*).

7. Groome, *Christian Religious Education*, 141–42.

the Spirit, and Responding to the Call. The value of their work is the intentionality given to the presence and role of the community in the process of spiritual formation. Cheryl Bridges-Johns' insights are equally expressed in her text, *Pentecostal Formation: Pedagogy Among the Oppressed* (1993), where the same four-movement grid is emphasized. This contribution emerges from her research in Latin American theology, where she focuses on a dialogue between Pentecostalism and the educational model of Paulo Friere.

Aspects of these components have been expressed by others in twentieth-century scholarship (seee Chart B on page 145). Barth, for example, referred to three components in the sharing of God's Word: proclamation (declaration), explication (explanation), and evangelical address (application).[8] Wells articulates three movements in evangelical circles as: confession (what is believed), reflection (a struggle with what it means to be a Christian), and a set of virtues or ethics (grounded in the confession and reflection).[9] Land's work in Pentecostal theology refers to the related elements of knowing, being, and doing.[10] Dash, Jackson, and Rasor, studying African-American theology, see similar features, which they name as: a liberating encounter, liberating reflection, and liberating action.[11] Butler is quoted in the Dash, Jackson, and Rasor work seeing these three elements as: what we know, what we feel, and what we do. Germane to Christian education, Edge translates these in the instructional arena as three primary goals of focus when crafting a Sunday School lesson: knowledge aims (imparting infor-

8. Barth, *Church Dogmatics* IV.3.2, 844–54.

9. Wells, *No Place for Truth*, 98.

10. Land, *Passion for the Kingdom*. Land's text makes this claim implicitly, while his course work and conversations make this position more explicit.

11. Dash, Jackson, Rasor, *Hidden Wholeness*, 5.

mation), inspiration aims (meaning is emphasized), and conduct aims (motivation to action is sought).[12]

Berlin argues the text itself influences readers in their readings;[13] she offers three steps in the analytical process: find textual features on which to base a reading; select those features that will become important in interpretation; and decide what to do with the selected features.[14] These share common ground with the aforementioned scholars, who also see, in assumed community contexts, an integrated process of observing, interpreting, and applying a text. Awareness of the biblical text's own design and how it's features shape or guide a reader, cannot be ignored in the hermeneutical process. As Berlin comments, "a hermeneutical system does not fully determine the meaning; rather, it channels the process whereby meaning is found."[15] The text in its final form is a statement to be heard by careful readers, and that statement from the text itself advances a reading method by which the text is introduced to us.

The foregoing survey is hardly comprehensive, yet this summary represents how interests in spiritual formation and theology see the need for a more informed and intentional approach to integrating elements of Christian experience and growth in the transformative process. The respective three movements cited in each example above correlate with movements two, three, and four in the reading I am proposing from the Esther story. In the above survey, however, a key element appears to be a "given": that being, the role of the reader and what she/he brings to a text. This element is linked to the role of the community as well.

12. Edge, *Teaching for Results*, vi–vii, 54–56.

13. Berlin, "The Role of the Text," 143.

14. Ibid., 145.

15. Ibid.

Each of the above researchers offers insight to the integration of features in the process of reading Scripture. Careful readers, however, must determine if the proposed grids offered above are imposed on Scripture or emerge from the structure and content of biblical literature itself. It is noted that none of the cited researchers specifically focuses on the genre of biblical narrative, and their proposed approaches to the reading process are applicable to all categories of biblical genre. One exception is the Johns and Bridges-Johns model intends a connection with aspects of the Gospel of John. Further, while the grids above are commensurate with the reading method proposed in this study, the contribution of this work seeks a clear reading method proposed by a particular biblical narrative itself. In much the same fashion as Deuteronomy 31:9–13 presupposes a community context of individuals of shared experience, an intentional reading of Torah, an exploration of meaning, and the imperative to live out what is learned from the text, the Esther story, though void of clear reference to Yahweh, follows a model given in the Scripture in guiding readers on how to read biblical stories.

The Esther story provides the parameters for reading biblical narrative, introducing the necessity of observational skills that define and are sensitive to the general components of narrative genre: characters and how a text shapes them (deeds, words, gender, and relationships to other story characters), how plot develops and moves toward crisis and resolution, the narrator's direct and indirect presence, and how characters are mouthpieces for the storyteller. Creating space geographically, quantitatively, and historically reflects on how a specific stage is an effective environment for particular words and deeds. The narrative space given to settings and characters demonstrates dominant priorities of an author's interests, providing a base for a reader's self-critique.

Asking "what readers bring to a text" couples with pedagogical concerns facilitating discovery. Lecture as the primary mode of instructional delivery gives way to a learning approach favoring dynamic dialogue about an individual's research (based on Esther's reading and discussion with Mordecai [ch. 4]). This shifts learning and ownership of values to student-centered analysis, reporting of findings, and exploration of options. The community dialogue fosters accountability to the primary text of study. Writing assignments serve as "mediators" of the learning process between mentor and student. To greater or lesser extent (and driven by the specific context of ministry), papers and brief, written reflection assignments carry the message between student and instructor, like Esther's maids and chamberlains (v. 4), Hatach (vv. 5, 6, 9, 10) and the like (vv. 12, 15).

Through verbal and written exercises, instructors become facilitators of discussion fostering interaction via a series of probing questions (v. 14). The educator is more a "tour guide" and less an "answer woman/man." The task is not accumulation of facts; rather, students reflect, respond, and react to the text in ways humanizing the subjective reader who is accountable to the text (without a stranglehold of unnecessary domination that chokes life out of what a text is saying to a student):

> If moreover, reading is a matter of historical importance, then Esther becomes a mirror for the contemporary critic. Like her, exposing the abuse of power, the danger of writing, and the instability of subjectivity, the critic can escape neither the responsibility for her activity nor the encapsulation of that activity in historically diverse, subjectless writing.[16]

16. Bal, "Lots of Writing," 95.

Hermeneutical Commitments

The Esther story's presence in Scripture avails itself to ministers in Christian service to the world. For such ministry, this project implies empowering readers with hermeneutical skills for engaging biblical narratives promotes faithful application of derived meanings. This reading highlights how one woman impacts a world given to patriarchal and ethnic slantedness. In Esther's example, readers move from a sense of naiveté to community solidarity, signaling a process of growth and transformation through reading Scripture.

As a genre for theological discourse, "story is the grammar of God, that is, if we take the literary genres in the Bible seriously."[17] The genre of biblical narrative invites students into a world often constituted differently from their own,[18] but into a world (that functions as a mirror) where they learn about themselves, and others, in the process of formation (Esther's background), information (her reading of a text), deformation (her struggles with the text), and transformation (her resolve). In the study of narrative art, the story reads the reader as much as it is read. Archer contends Scripture is the meta-narrative that "must master the reader and this needs to be based on the narrative's terms."[19] While Bakhtin avoids static (single-meaning) views of texts, the function of narrative to self-express and self-critique (Amit) the needs and values of a faith community is not ignored. We reflect what we value/devalue in our curricular commitments. Like Esther, we face a decision: insulation in a "safe" illusion of the kingdom or risky steps toward solidarity in our readings. Reading biblical narratives "invite[s] us to read scripture for its capacity to rescue us from individualism so that we might see and live our individuality in the

17. Archer, "Pentecostal Hermeneutics," 11.

18. Amit, *Reading Biblical Narratives*, 33.

19. Archer, 12.

context of community."[20] Faithful readings of texts precede informed exploration of social implications or theological stances. In environments given to only one form or method of reading, the potential for self-discovery and informed, contextualized ministry is hindered. Equipping students to read this genre is incumbent upon Christian education efforts if its goal of adequate ministerial preparation is taken seriously. Ignoring the power of story in neglected texts of any given curriculum is really a flexing once more of the hegemonious control of the narrative's Persian Empire, and a "silencing" of those (people, books) deemed weak in its midst. The power of narrative refuses to be controlled and silenced, and will be given voice, albeit vicariously, to the deconstruction of singular modes of thought and course design.

20. Goldingay, "Biblical Story," 8

4

Conclusion

"The critic reading 'Esther' cannot innocently submit to lots."[1]

—Mieke Bal

WHAT WILL future researchers say of the twenty-first century? Will the telltale signs of narrative in written and dramatic forms display an apologetic of our craving for good literature and entertainment? Will the prolonged periods and protracted stare-offerings we pay in homage to TV sets, or the proliferation of novels we read represent the sum of our lives, beliefs, and worship? Given the human proclivity toward narrative, will emphases on story be detected or detached in ministerial efforts? Will the record show Christian education efforts delighted in or diminished narrative readings?

Biblical narrative deserves greater sensitivity, space, and status in efforts of quality Christian ministry. Contending for story's power over imbalances produced by emphasis on other reading methods, or treatments reducing the text to little more than merely trite thought, Archer asserts:

> Narrative is story and as a story it creates a world in which the reader may dwell. Narrative

1. Bal, "Lots of Writing," 96.

> invites the reader to create and discover meaning. Reducing the story to some moral principle seems to imply that the narrative portions of Scripture are not effective means in and of themselves by which a community's identity can be shaped or challenged. Thus, principalizing emphasizes the notion that "narrative is a relatively unimportant moral category" which sees "stories" as illustrations of some deeper truth that we can understand and should learn to articulate in a non-narrative mode.[2]

Sundberg further observes, "Many students go into the ministry wounded by their academic experience and weakened in their ability to offer a vigorous witness to the truth they hold."[3] Christian education agents must review their curriculum (and its effects), asking if courses, classes, and conduct (methods) are adequately equipping women and men of diverse backgrounds, and ministry contexts, to meet the challenges posed in the cultural settings where they (intend to) serve. To reach a North American, English-speaking body of readers, curriculum designs will take on particular shapes. However, as missionaries, teachers, preachers, and a host of spiritually gifted ministers find themselves called to various people-groups and unique situations, it is incumbent we explore the adequacy of tools students take with them to answer their callings. As a corrective to the neglect of studies in biblical narrative, encountering the text on its own merits is an initial step bridging historical-critical interests and a lived faith:

> Relishing the Bible as literature offers a new, more realistic path to the power of Scripture

2. Archer, "Pentecostal Hermeneutics," 10–11.

3. Bartholomew, Green, and Moller, *Renewing Biblical Interpretation*, 77.

> and a new path to authority. By reducing the historical distance between us and the text and by removing the necessity of knowing who the author is, biblical authors become our siblings who share human experience through the common capacity to appreciate literature.[4]

Developing courses in reading biblical narrative is a significant supplement to the ministerial task. The power, language, and crafting of story influence pedagogical interests, shaping course design and instructional methods.

Goldingay asserts hero stories "form a characteristic resource for minorities under pressure."[5]As readers so define themselves in an ever-changing world of circumstances, Esther's character development in her story world models how readers are read in the process of their own transformation—a process facilitated in the careful engagement with biblical narrative. While the Esther story lacks clear reference to God, "the storyteller . . . as an artist makes Yahweh conspicuous by his absence."[6] Such unique features of the text invite exploration into the crafting of biblical story and examination of character sketches. Alter observes:

> The biblical tale, through the most rigorous economy of means, leads us again and again to ponder complexities of motive and ambiguities of character, because these are essential aspects of its vision of man [*sic*] created by God, enjoying or suffering the consequences of human freedom.[7]

The lens through which one reads colors, clarifies, or skews the story. We have the capacity to read and communicate,

4. Campbell, "Relishing the Bible," 815.
5. Goldingay, *Israel's Gospel*, 772.
6. Clines, "Story and Poem," 121.
7. Alter, *The Art of Biblical Narrative*, 22.

though Mitchell asserts there is no "formula for communication."[8] We learn from the Esther narrative that the variety of characters is an array or whole host of readers.[9] In a world where men tell women what to do, it is significant Esther is a thinking individual who reads a text and reaches conclusions after meaningful dialogue (4:8, 16–17). In the case of narrative, a single formula or method might mean there is only one way to read Esther—and what if that one is Haman's?! Thus, it is not bad news there is no formula for communication, if this means a freedom to read from diverse vantages that are faithful to the text.

While "the beauty of a good story is its openness—the way you or I or anyone reading it can take it in and use it for ourselves"[10]—the *hermeneut* (interpreter) is to distinguish between readings that serve selfish outcomes versus those faithful to, and representative of, features of the biblical text. Readers who engage biblical narrative through inductive study may (in some contexts) adopt an unconventional reading method. While risky, inductive readings, which integrate an awareness of what readers bring to texts, engage the literature, wrestle with meaning(s), and apply learned values in faithful community-living, foster life in the place of a mindless slavery to entrenched reading methods. Without demeaning the etiology of Purim and focusing on how the Esther story opens up multiple reasons for reading and holding readers accountable to the ethics of interpersonal interaction, portions of Bal's argument are insightful:

> Had Mordecai and Esther been as blind as Haman, they would have been inadequate readers, powerless to exploit the delay of writing. . . . For when the lot has determined that

8. Mitchell, "Why Care About Stories?" 32.

9. See again, Bal.

10. Mitchell, 32.

> another people is now subject to danger, the critic reading "Esther" cannot innocently submit to lots. . . . By reading the text as about reading-writing, one is led to reflect upon all the issues intricated with it: gender, power, and the state, genocide and otherness, submission and agency. In short, upon history.[11]

The Esther narrative tells how a countercultural queen's effectiveness as a reader saw many converted to, or identified with, the Jews (8:17); her people are recipients of liberation. Without proselytizing, readers can identify with this story of Jewish struggle. As the narrative's mirror reads us, we find pause to analyze how we will respond when faced with our own struggles, or how we will act when confronted with the plight of others. Readers are thus forced to a decision regarding their commitments to reading methods: Is there adequate room for reading biblical narrative in our efforts of Christian ministry, or is this reading practice (and narrative) relegated to the "king's house" (1:9)?

Rabbinic thought says one day all of the Jewish feasts will cease, but Purim is eternal (celebrating everlasting deliverance in the reversing of life's tragedies). For narrative studies, there is perpetual reason to constantly celebrate if the liberation of the Esther story informs our reading commitments. Mitchell observes:

> If Christianity is to be more than an object we know *about*, if it has passionate elements about it, if it is a life-view and not simply a phenomenon, then we have need of the kind of communication that leads to self-reflection.[12]

11. Bal, 96.

12. Mitchell, 42. Further, "If stories have a moral implication, it is that readers need to accept each other with their human moral weakness. The absence of moral judgments from the stories draws

Reading biblical narrative does just that. To further marginalize reading biblical narrative in any context of Christian ministry is to oppress Vashti and Esther once more.

---

readers into them to make their own judgments as they set these stories alongside the stories of their own lives" (Goldingay, *Israel's Gospel*, 287).

Appendix 1

Study Questions on the Text of Esther

A SERIES of questions are offered below as a start toward examination of the book of Esther as a whole. The questions are designed to help readers begin the process of interviewing passages of Scripture with an emphasis on discerning facts without imposing interpretive presuppositions. Sensitivity is given foremost to literary aspects of the text; social relationships, historical factors, and theological practices surfacing in this story world.

This set of questions is not meant to be exhaustive. They intend to foster an awareness of basic facts found in the text itself, serving as discussion starters in group study. These initial points of inquiry also function as a foundation for the framing of observations in appendix 2, collectively focused on narrative qualities in appendix 3. Each chapter is treated as a unique scene in the larger narrative as a whole, with relationships drawn between the chapters at key points. A section summary of narrative qualities will be developed near the end of each chapter's study questions.

Esther Chapter 1

1. Who is speaking in verses 1–14?
2. During what time does the narrator indicate the story transpires? (v. 1)
3. Who is the monarch referenced at the outset of the story? (v. 1)
4. How is the vastness of this monarch's kingdom described? (v. 1)
5. Where is the headquarters of this kingdom? (v. 2)
6. What did this king do in the third year of his reign? (v. 3)
7. List all those present at this event. (v. 3).
8. How long did this event last? (v. 4)
9. What did Xerxes display during this time? (v. 4)
10. When these days were past, what did Xerxes do next? (v. 5)
11. How long did this event last? (v. 5)
12. Where was this banquet held? (v. 5)
13. Who attended this banquet? (v. 5)
14. Describe the garden setting of this banquet in detail. (v. 6)
15. What was served during this banquet? (v. 7)
16. How does the writer describe the drinking cups? (v. 7)

17. How does the writer describe the quantity of wine available at this banquet? (v. 7)

18. What did the king command regarding the banquet? (v. 8)

19. Who also held a banquet? (v. 9)

20. Who attended this banquet? (v. 9)

21. Where was this banquet held? (v. 9)

22. Note the titles of reference for the two named characters in verse 9.

23. How many banquets have been held in verses 1–8?

24. Compare and contrast the banquets of verses 1–8 with the banquet of verse 9; what is unique about each setting.

25. How is the king described on the seventh day of this second banquet? (v. 10)

26. What does the king do on the seventh day of this banquet? (vv. 10–11)

27. How many eunuchs are commanded in verse 10?

28. List the names given for these eunuchs. (v. 10)

29. What does the king command of these eunuchs? (v. 11)

30. What specifically is Queen Vashti to wear when she appears before the king? (v. 11)

31. What is the purpose for calling the queen? (v. 11)

32. How is the queen's appearance described? (v. 11)
33. Does the text define what "beauty" is? (v. 11)
34. Do the attendants deliver the king's message to the queen? (v. 12)
35. How does the queen respond? (v. 12).
36. Who indicates the queen's response? (v. 12)
37. What is the king's reaction? (v. 12)
38. Does time lapse between verses 12 and 13?
39. What custom is referenced? (v. 13)
40. List the names of the wise men the king consulted. (v. 14)
41. How could the king convene a meeting of the wise advisors so quickly? (vv. 13–14; see also v. 3)
42. How many wise men are referenced in this passage? (v. 14)
43. Who is the last named counselor in this list? (v. 14)
44. List the brief résumé of three qualities given for these wise men (v. 14).
45. Who speaks in verse 15?
46. What is asked of these counselors? (v. 15)
47. Why is this question asked? (v. 15)
48. Who replies to the question? (v. 16)

49. In what setting does Memucan respond? (v. 16)

50. Who does Memucan say Queen Vashti as offended? (v. 16)

51. What does Memucan rationalize will happen? (v. 17–18)

52. Does Memucan cite any written law that the queen has violated? (vv. 17–18)

53. Is there any record of specific quotes from the queen? (vv. 1–18).

54. Who supplies information of the queen's response? (vv. 12, 17–18)

55. What does Memucan propose be done? (v. 19)

56. Why does Memucan suggest the king "write" a law? (v. 19)

57. How is Vashti referred to in verse 17? How is she referred to in verse 19?

58. What does Memucan's proposal hope to offset? (compare vv. 18 and 20)

59. How does reference to "from the least to the greatest" echo the stage set in verse 1?

60. How is Memucan's proposal received? (v. 21)

61. Who supplies this information on the acceptance of Memucan's idea? (v. 21)

62. What does the king do? (vv. 21–22)

63. What does the king command in verse 22? How is this similar to verse 8?

64. Narrator:

    a. Observe and record each instance where the narrator is speaking.

    b. Also note where the narrator uses characters to speak in the process of conveying the story.

65. Characters:

    a. List all the characters in the passage.

    b. Next, identify any information in the passage that defines the character (look for actions, words, descriptions, emotions, rank, etc.). Begin building a résumé for each character.

66. Plot:

    a. How does the story begin?

    b. What crisis or challenge mounts as the story line progresses?

    c. How is the crisis resolved?

67. Setting:

    a. Describe the stage or setting where the story takes place.

    b. Define the setting(s) in terms of the historical period as well as broad or local stages where the actors play their roles.

68. Time:

    a. What time references are given in this chapter?

    b. Is there mention of a historical period?

    c. Are there specific time references or mention of the passage of time? Cite these.

    d. How are lapses in time inferred for events to transpire?

69. Style:

    a. How is the story told?

    b. What words or themes are chosen to convey meaning? How do these repeat in the passage?

    c. How is the environment or stage cast by giving eight verses of attention to the men's parties and only one verse to the women's celebration?

Esther Chapter 2

1. Who is speaking or providing the information in chapter 2?

2. How is a lapse or passing of time mentioned in verse 1?

3. How is the king referred to, and how is the queen referred to in verse 1?

4. What do the attendants propose? (v. 2)

5. How is this proposal a continuation of Memucan's advice? (see 1:19)

6. Who is to be appointed to carry out this proposal? (2:3)

7. How many provinces are there for these appointments? (2:3; 1:1)

8. From where, and to where, are the young virgins brought? (2:3)

9. How is this proposal of verse 3 similar to the events of 1:1–4 and then 1:5–8?

10. Who is to care for those gathered and brought to Susa? (2:3)

11. What is Hegai's résumé? (v. 3)

12. How will the virgins be treated? (v. 3)

13. What will the outcome be for the one girl who pleases the king? (v. 4)

14. Who will she replace? (v. 4)

15. How does the king respond to the idea? (v. 4)

16. How is the king's response similar to the advice of his counselors in 1:21–22?

17. Where is the king when he remembers and is advised by his attendants? (1:5; 2:3)

18. How many edicts has the king dispatched so far in the story? (1:19–22; 2:8)

19. Where does the narrator refer to when introducing the next character? (2:5)

20. What is Mordecai's résumé? (vv. 5–6)

21. What is inferred about the passage of time in verse 6? (Note: Who had taken Jerusalem captive? Yet, who now controls the kingdom? See 1:3)

22. What is the relationship of Mordecai to Esther? (2:7)

23. What is Esther's résumé? (v. 7)

24. How is Esther's beauty defined? (v. 7)

25. Compare Esther's beauty to Vashti's beauty (2:7; 1:11)

26. How has the edict (2:1–4) been carried out? (v. 8)

27. Does the narrator indicate any choice on the part of the girls who are gathered to go to the king? (vv. 2, 7–8)

28. Who alone, of all those gathered, is named in verse 8?

29. How is general information (v. 8a) made specific (v. 8b)?

30. How does this reflect the style of:

    a. 1:1

    b. 1:1–4 and 1:5–8

    c. 2:3

31. How is Esther referred to impersonally in 2:9?

32. How quickly does the narrator get to the point of Hegai's estimation of Esther? (v. 9)

33. What does Hegai say? (v. 9)

34. Rather, what does Hegai do? (v. 9)

35. What information does the narrator specifically call to the reader's attention about Esther's nationality and background? (v. 10)

36. Who had forbidden Esther to reveal this information? (v. 10)

37. What other information is supplied in verse 11 regarding Mordecai's care for Esther?

38. How is time referenced in verse 11 regarding Mordecai's tracking of Esther?

39. What stage or setting is referred to in verse 11 for Mordecai's actions?

40. What process does the narrator say the gathered virgins went through before their night with the king? (v. 12)

41. How long was each beauty treatment? (v. 12)

42. How many treatments are referred to? (v. 12)

43. How does this reflect the narrator's style of telling events in doublets (or twos)? For a sampling, see:

    a. 1:1–4 and 1:5–8

    b. 1:5–8 and 1:9

c. 1:8 and 1:22

d. 1:21 and 2:4

44. How does the virgin then go the king? (2:13)

45. What happened after she spent the night with the king? (v. 14)

46. How many "parts" of the harem are inferred in this passage? (vv. 8, 14)

47. How many caretakers were in charge of the women? (vv. 8, 14)

48. What was required for the woman to see the king again? (v. 14)

49. How many women have been named so far in the text? (1:8; 2:7)

50. At a minimum, how much time lapsed before Esther went to the king in 2:15? (v. 12)

51. What background information does the narrator repeat regarding Esther's heritage? (v. 15)

52. What does Esther take with her for her one night with the king? (vv. 13, 15)

53. How do the people react to Esther? (v. 15)

54. How is time referenced for Esther's meeting with Xerxes? (v. 15)

55. How does the king react to Esther? (v. 17)

56. What does the king do to Esther? (v. 17)

57. In response to selecting a queen, what does Xerxes do? (v. 18)

58. What is this banquet called? (v. 18)

59. Who celebrates at this banquet? (compare 2:18 and 1:3)

60. What does Xerxes do in tandem with this banquet? (v. 18)

61. Even though a queen is chosen (v. 17), what event transpires next? (v. 19)

    a. How many times have girls been gathered? (vv. 8, 19)

    b. What does the narrator remind readers of? (vv. 10, 20)

    c. Where is Mordecai stationed in the narrative? (vv. 11, 19)

    d. What does the event of verse 19 suggest about the passage of time?

62. While at the king's gate (v. 21) what does Mordecai uncover? (v. 22)

63. Who were the two conspirators against the king? (v. 21)

64. What does Mordecai do with the information? (v. 22)

65. How does Esther report the information? (v. 22)

66. What specifically happens to the conspirators? (v. 23)

67. What happens to this information regarding Mordecai's help to the king? (v. 23)

68. Narrator:

    a. How is the narrator present in this passage?

    b. What speeches are given by characters (through which the narrator speaks)?

69. Characters:

    a. Who are the characters referred to in this passage?

    b. Who are new characters? What is learned about them?

    c. Which are named? Which are unnamed?

    d. For characters already introduced in chapter 1, what new information is added to their résumé(s) in this chapter?

70. Plot:

    a. What issues surface in this chapter raising a sense of conflict? (Note: There may be more than one conflict context or issue to deal with.)

    b. What begins the conflict?

    c. Where does the conflict reach a pinnacle?

    d. How is the challenge or issue resolved?

71. Setting:

    a. What settings are referred to in this chapter?

    b. Which of these are rooted in chapter 1?

    c. Which are new settings that develop information from chapter 1?

72. Time:

    a. What historical period(s) is referred to in the chapter?

    b. How specifically is the Babylonian exile of the Jews referenced?

    c. How is time or the movement of time specifically documented?

    d. How is the movement of time suggested in the events or actions of the chapter?

73. Style:

    a. What stylistics devices does the narrator use to reinforce themes of chapter 1?

    b. What word choices or events offer a sense of gravity to the events of chapter 2?

    c. How does naming or not naming characters personalize or depersonalize them?

    d. What effect does reference to the Babylonian exile have on painting Esther as displaced territorially and ethnically?

e. How does this sense of Esther's displacement shape her character further as an orphan and as a young woman?

Esther Chapter 3

1. How is time referred to in verse 1?
2. Which new character is introduced in verse 1?
3. Who introduces and honors this new character? (v. 1)
4. Why is Haman honored? (v. 1)
5. What is known of his background? (v. 1)
6. How does the king honor Haman? (v. 1)
7. How do the people respond to Haman? (v. 2a)
8. How does Mordecai respond to Haman? (v. 2b)
9. What do the royal officials ask Mordecai? (v. 3)
10. Does Mordecai offer any recorded response to their question? (v. 3)
11. How long do the royal officials persist in questioning Mordecai? (v. 4)
12. Does Mordecai ever bow to Haman? (v. 4)
13. What do the royal officials do next? (v. 4)
14. What feature of Mordecai's résumé is specifically singled out in their report? (v. 4)

15. What does Haman investigate? (v. 5)

16. What is Haman's response to Mordecai? (v. 5)

17. What Jewish tribe is Mordecai associated with? (2:5)

18. Why does Mordecai refuse to bow to Haman? (3:5)

    The passage does not indicate why Mordecai would not bow to Haman. Readers are encouraged to explore the biblical background of the Amalekites by reading Exodus 17:8–16; Deuteronomy 25:17–19; and Saul's failure with Agag, king of the Amalekites in 1 Samuel 15. Note Saul's family tribe (1 Samuel 9:1–2).

19. What did Haman learn of Mordecai's background? (3:6)

20. What does Haman plot? (v. 6)

21. What was cast in Haman's presence to select a date for extermination of the Jews? (v. 7)

22. When did this casting take place? (v. 7)

23. On what day did the lot fall? (v. 7)

24. When Haman met with Xerxes, what did he report? (v. 8)

25. Does Haman reveal the precise identity of these people in his report? (vv. 8–9)

26. Does Xerxes ask about the identity of this people? (vv. 8–11)

27. What does Haman inform the king about these people? (v. 8)

28. What does Haman propose the king sanction? (v. 9)

29. How much is Haman willing to personally donate to the cause? (v. 9)

30. What does the king do in response to Haman's proposal? (v. 10)

31. How is Haman's background contrasted to the identity of the Jews? (v. 10)

32. What does Xerxes say to Haman? (v. 11)

33. How does this scene further paint Xerxes' interest in money and people? (v. 11)

34. When are the royal secretaries summoned? (v. 12)

35. What are they commissioned to write? (v. 12)

36. How is the authority of the edict emphasized? (v. 12)

37. What three actions against the Jews does Haman order in the name of the king? (v. 13)

38. Who exactly among the Jews will be targeted? (v. 13)

39. When will this action be carried out? (v. 13)

40. What will be done with their goods? (v. 13)

41. What was issued as law? (v. 14)

42. How many edicts have now been issued in the king's name?

    a. 1:21–22; 2:8; 3:15

    b. How is 2:8 different from the other two edicts?

43. What do the king and Haman do after the dispatch? (3:15)

44. How is this action similar to events in 1:7–8? (If the "banquets" of 1:1–4 and 2:18 include drinking, include these passages as well in your assessment of 3:15.)

45. How do the people of Susa respond to the king's edict? (3:15)

46. Narrator:

    a. In what way(s) is the narrator present in this passage supplying information?

    b. In what way(s) is the story told through characters?

47. Characters:

    a. Which character(s) continues from chapters 1 and 2 into chapter 3?

    b. Which character(s) is new in chapter 3? Construct background information on the new character(s).

48. Plot:

    a. What plot elements begin in this chapter?

b. How does tension mount?

c. Is there any resolve to this conflict yet?

49. Setting:

    a. What setting(s) forms the backdrop for the events of this passage?

    b. Who are the key players in each setting/scene?

50. Time:

    a. In what way(s) is time specifically referenced?

    b. In what way(s) is time inferred to be passing?

51. Style:

    a. What background stories might the narrator use to cast the tension between the characters?

    b. How are themes or places from chapters 1 and 2 used in chapter 3?

Esther Chapter 4

1. What information came to Mordecai? (4:1; 3:14–15)

2. How does Mordecai respond to the news? (4:1)

3. How far does Mordecai take his protest? (v. 2)

4. What is the response of the Jews in the outlying provinces? (v. 3)

5. How is the reaction of Mordecai and that of his people similar? (vv. 1–3)

6. Who carries news to Esther? (v. 4)

7. What is told to her? (v. 4)

8. What does Esther do? (v. 4)

9. How does Mordecai respond to Esther's gift of clothing? (v. 4)

10. Who does Esther summon and what does she order him to do? (v. 5)

11. How is this action different for Esther's character? (v. 5)

    a. Notice what she was told and who commanded her in 2:10 and 2:20.

    b. Observe who guided Esther's choice in 2:15.

    c. She gives credit to another in 2:22.

12. How does Hatach respond in 4:6?

13. Where is Mordecai now located? (v. 6)

14. What does Mordecai relay to Esther through Hatach? (v. 7)

15. What details of the arrangement did Mordecai know about? (4:7; 3:9)

16. What did Mordecai give to Hatach? (4:8a; 3:14–15)

17. What was Hatach to do with this copy? (4:8b)

18. What proposal does Mordecai urge of Esther? (v. 8b)

19. What does Hatach do? (v. 9)

20. What is Esther's response? (vv. 10–11)

    a. What law or protocol is well known in the kingdom? (v. 11)

    b. What is the penalty for appearing before the king without a summons? (2:14; 4:11)

    c. What is the only exception to this law? (4:11)

    d. How long has it been since Esther had been called to the king? (v. 11)

21. Who likely carried Esther's response back to Mordecai in verse 12? (see v. 5)

22. Who likely carried Mordecai's response back to Esther (see vv. 5, 12, etc.)

23. How does Mordecai respond to Esther's objections? (vv. 13–14)

    a. Does Mordecai address the possibility of Esther escaping harm? (v. 13)

    b. Is Mordecai hopeful that deliverance will come whether Esther acts or not? (v. 14)

    c. How does Mordecai point out the possible purpose of Esther's role as queen? (v. 14)

24. Who likely carried Esther's response back to Mordecai in verse 15? (see vv. 5, 12, etc.)

25. Note, Esther again commands a man in verse 16 (see also v. 5).

    a. What does Esther call upon Mordecai to do?

    b. What does Esther pledge to do?

    c. What does Esther again remind Mordecai of? (vv. 11, 16)

26. What does Mordecai do in response? (v. 17)

27. Narrator:

    a. How is the narrator present in telling the events of this scene?

    b. How does the narrator effectively use characters in telling the element of this part of the story?

28. Characters:

    a. Who are the primary characters of this chapter?

    b. What is known of these characters that come forward from prior chapters?

    c. What new words or actions transpire that indicate a change or development in the character's makeup?

    d. Who is a new character introduced in this passage? How does this character function?

29. Plot:

    a. What is the ongoing crisis that informs the tension of this chapter?

b. How is tension mounting at this point in the story?

c. What elements are introduced to raise the plot's tension?

d. What are the aspects of challenge that factor into making this tension an issue of concern for each of the characters in dialogue?

e. What limited resolve has Esther reached at this point?

30. Setting:

a. Where do these conversations take place?

b. How are the concerns of the Jews, both broad (kingdom at large) and local (in Susa), shared in this chapter?

31. Time:

a. How has time been referenced in this passage?

b. How has time moved or lapsed in this story?

c. How is the lapse of time inferred in the carrying of messages back and forth?

d. What specific amount of time has Esther called for in her preparation to meet the king?

e. How does this function as a delay in order the raise the pitch of the plot?

32. Style:

    a. How effective is the use of Hatach's name, or not using his name, in the transfer of information between Esther and Mordecai?

    b. How does Esther's commanding men in this passage signal a change in her character from prior scenes?

Esther Chapter 5

1. How long after the conversation with Mordecai (ch. 4) does Esther act? (5:1)
2. How does this reference to time relate to her conversation with Mordecai? (4:16)
3. What precisely does Esther do? (5:1)
4. Where does Esther stand? (v. 1)
5. Where is the king? (v. 1)
6. What is the threat at this point in the narrative? (4:11)
7. How does the king respond? (5:2)
8. What does the king ask? (v. 3)
9. What does the king pledge to Esther? (v. 3)
10. What is Esther's request? (v. 4)
11. When will her banquet be held? (v. 4)
12. Who specifically is invited to attend Esther's banquet? (v. 4)

13. Up to this point in the narrative, who has given banquets? (see 1:1–8 and 2:18)

    a. In chapter 1, what was the relationship of the men's party to that of the women's? (compare 1:1–8 to 1:9)

    b. How is this action of Esther like the change of her character witnessed in chapter 4?

14. How does the request of Esther "delay" getting to the real issue of her concern? (5:4)

15. What order does the king issue? (v. 5)

16. Who supplies the information that the king and Haman attended Esther's banquet? (v. 5b)

17. What question does the king ask Esther again? (v. 6)

18. What was the king doing when this question is asked? (v. 6a)

19. How is this action like other occasions the king is seen in? (see 1:1–8; 2:18; 3:15)

20. What pledge does the king give to Esther a second time? (5:6)

21. What response does Esther give to the king? (vv. 7–8)

22. How does Esther "delay" the king a second time? (vv. 7–8)

23. Who specifically is to attend the second banquet? (v. 8)

24. What does Esther promise she will reveal at the second banquet? (v. 8)

25. When will the second banquet be held? (v. 8)

26. What is Haman's state of mind at the two invitations? (v. 9)

27. What does the site of Mordecai do to Haman? (v. 9)

28. How does Mordecai continue to act toward Haman? (v. 9)

29. Where does Haman go next? (v. 10)

30. What does Haman do at home? (vv. 10–13)

31. Who is Zeresh? (v. 10)

32. How many women are named in the story to this point?

    a. 1:9

    b. 2:7

    c. 5:10

33. How does Haman's action in 5:10 accord with information given in 1:11, 1:22, and 2:14?

34. Of what does Haman boast? (5:11–12)

35. Is Haman satisfied with his accomplishments? (v. 13)

36. How many times is this aspect of Haman's character highlighted? (vv. 9–13)

37. Who gives advice to Haman on how to handle Mordecai? (v. 14)

38. What do they propose? (v. 14)

39. How tall were gallows to be? (v. 14)

    a. How tall do gallows have to be in order to execute Mordecai?

    b. Compare this detail to the information given in 2:23 regarding the execution of the two assassins.

40. Compare the structure of elements (problem, counselors, proposal, outcome) in 5:14 with:

    a. 1:12–21

    b. 2:1–4

    c. Chapter 4

41. Narrator:

    a. At what specific points does the narrator speak?

    b. At what specific points does the narrator speak through the characters?

42. Characters:

    a. Who are the named and primary characters of these two scenes in chapter 5?

    b. Who is new to the cast of characters?

    c. What information is given for each character that continues to define their respective roles?

43. Plot:

    a. What is the crisis or challenge opening the chapter?

    b. How is this immediate challenge resolved?

    c. What is the next challenge posed in the chapter?

    d. What proposal is given to resolve this conflict?

44. Setting:

    a. Where does Esther's initial meeting with the king take place?

    b. What does she propose the king and Haman attend?

    c. In what setting does she promise to reveal her real request?

    d. Where does Mordecai sit?

    e. Where does Haman go to meet with his friends and wife?

45. Time:

    a. What periods of time are specifically mentioned in the passage?

    b. What aspects of the text indicate time is passing, though not specifically mentioned?

46. Style:

    a. What elements of the narrative in this chapter are similar to aspects of how the story has been told in prior chapters?

    b. How does the writer use "delay" to heighten the tone of the plot?

    c. Is the king ever named in this passage?

    d. How does the exaggeration of seventy-five-foot gallows (5:14) serve as an attempt to "outdo" the king (2:23)?

Esther Chapter 6

1. How has time lapsed from the events in chapter 5 to the opening of chapter 6? (6:1)

2. What does the king order during his insomnia? (v. 1)

3. How does this action recall the information given in 2:22–23?

4. What does Xerxes hear during the reading? (6:2)

5. What does Xerxes ask in response? (v. 3a)

6. What do his unnamed attendants tell him? (v. 3b)

7. What is Xerxes' second question? (v. 4a)

8. Who does the narrator indicate has just entered the court? (v. 4b)

9. Why has Haman arrived so early at the king's court? (5:14; 6:4b)

10. How long has the king been listening to the reading of the chronicles? (6:1–4; 5:14)

11. Who do the attendants reinforce is in the outer court? (6:4b, 5)

12. What does the king command? (v. 5b)

13. What does the king ask Haman? (v. 6a)

14. What does Haman assume? (v. 6b)

15. What specifically does Haman propose in response to the king's question? (v. 7–9)

    a. What does Haman want to wear? (v. 8a)

    b. What does Haman want to ride? (vv. 8b–9)

    c. What does Haman want to hear? (v. 9)

16. How does the king respond to this proposal? (v. 10)

17. Does Haman do exactly as the king has commanded? (v. 11)

18. What has Mordecai said during this entire episode? (vv. 11–12)

19. How does this shame Haman? (v. 12)

20. Where does Mordecai return to? (v. 12)

21. Where does Haman go? (v. 12)

22. What is Haman's attire as he returns home? (v. 12b)

23. What does Haman report? (v. 13a)

24. Who does he tell? (v. 13a)

25. How do his advisors and his wife Zeresh respond? (v. 13b)

26. What aspect of Mordecai's background do they point to? (v. 13b)

27. What do Haman's counselors indicate will be his end? (v. 13b)

While the NIV uses "ruin," the KJV stresses "fall." The exchange is a delightful wordplay: Mordecai who would not bow (or fall) is contrasted to Haman who will fall. Look for additional connections to the theme of "rising and falling" in the text.

28. What transpires at the same time they are counseling Haman? (v. 14)

29. Narrator:

    a. How is the narrator present in this chapter?

    b. Where do the actions and speeches of the characters take over as the narrator recedes into the background?

30. Characters:

    a. Who are the primary characters in this chapter?

    b. Who are the supporting cast of characters in this chapter?

c. What actions and speeches are outlined in the passage?

d. How do these actions and speeches shape the characters?

31. Plot:

a. What is the crisis or concern of Haman?

b. What is the crisis or concern of Xerxes?

c. What is the ongoing crisis or concern of Mordecai?

d. How do these three challenges collide in chapter 6?

32. Setting:

a. Where does Haman meet with the king?

b. Where does Haman propose the "man the king delights to honor" be recognized?

c. Where does Haman honor Mordecai?

d. Where does Mordecai return to?

e. Where does Haman go in shame?

f. What is the next setting anticipated at the end of the chapter?

33. Time:

a. How has time been effectively framed in the night-to-day movement of events?

b. How long did it take for the king to learn of Mordecai's help to the kingdom?

c. How long might it have taken for Haman to meet with the king?

d. How long might it have taken for Haman to carry out the king's command and honor Mordecai?

e. Observe how a time lapse is inferred in Haman's travel back to his home and reporting of the day's events.

f. Note how swiftly the narrator indicates Haman is taken to his appointment with the king and queen.

g. How has chapter 6 as a whole framed a "delay" between the appointment set in 5:7–8 and 7:1–2?

34. Style:

a. What is odd about Haman immediately seeking the life of Mordecai? (see 3:12–15; 5:9; 6:4)

b. How has irony been effectively used in this passage?

Esther Chapter 7

1. Who supplies the details of verse 1?

2. What title of honor is given to . . .

    a. Xerxes (inferred but not named in v. 2)
    b. Esther (v. 2)
    c. Haman (v. 2) [Note: There is no honor given him here.]

3. What are the three main characters doing? (v. 2)
    a. How does this action differ from 1:1–8 and 1:9?
    b. How is this action similar to 5:6–8?
4. What pledge does the king reiterate for a third time? (7:2)
    a. Recall what has he promised in 5:3.
    b. Note what he vowed a second time in 5:6.
5. How does Esther answer the king? (7:3)
    a. How does this response differ from 5:4?
    b. How does this response differ from 5:8?
6. How does Esther identify herself in 7:3?
7. What has she previously kept hidden? (2:10)
8. What is the crisis that Esther and her people face? (7:3)
9. What three specific things does Esther see are planned for her and her people? (v. 4)
10. Who is Esther quoting in verse 4? (3:13)

11. What titles of royalty are used in 7:5 to accent the theme of authority?

12. What does the king ask? (v. 5)

13. Who does Esther pinpoint as the perpetrator? (v. 6)

14. How does Esther describe Haman to the king? (v. 6)

15. How is her declaration in verse 6 more specific than Haman's request of 3:8?

16. How does Haman respond to this news? (7:6b)

17. How does the king respond to this news? (v. 7a)

    a. What has the king previously done with Haman? (3:1, 15)

    b. What does the king now leave? (7:7)

18. Where does the king go? (v. 7b)

19. What does Haman realize? (v. 7b)

20. What does Haman do? (v. 7b)

21. What does the king see when he returns? (v. 8)

22. What does the king say? (v. 8)

23. Is this an accurate assessment of what Haman is actually doing? (v. 8a)

24. How is Haman's posture a fulfillment of Zeresh's foresight? (see 6:13)

25. How is Haman shamed again? (7:8b)

26. What information does Harbona report to the king? (v. 9a)

27. What details are included in Harbona's report? (v. 9)

28. What order does the king give? (v. 9b)

    a. What problem has the king previously had? (1:13–15)

    b. In contrast, how has the king previously acted toward Haman? (3:1)

29. What happens to Haman? (7:10)

    a. What had been planned for Mordecai in 6:4?

    b. Ironically, what happened to Mordecai in 6:10?

    c. In similar fashion, what was the purpose of Haman's gallows? (5:14)

    d. However, what transpired on these gallows? (7:10)

30. What is the king's emotional state following Haman's execution? (v. 10)

31. Narrator:

    a. What information does the narrator supply directly in this chapter?

    b. Who are the primary speakers to whom the narrator gives voice?

32. Characters:

    a. Name the characters who are primary actors in this scene.

    b. Who are supporting characters in this passage?

33. Plot:

    a. What crisis faces Haman?

    b. How does this scene continue events introduced in chapter 6?

    c. What crisis does Esther and her people face?

    d. What dilemma does the king have to deal with?

    e. What "resolution" is there to the immediate crisis of Haman challenging the life of the queen?

    f. Does Haman's death on his own gallows negate the threat to the Jewish people?

34. Setting:

    a. What is the stage or setting for Esther's revelation of identity?

    b. Where does the king go when he hears the news of Haman's plot?

    c. To where does the king return?

    d. Where does Esther sit and Haman fall?

e. What setting does Harbona describe to the king?

f. Where is Haman executed?

35. Time:

a. What time sequence is the setting for this banquet? (7:2)

b. How do the actions of the king hearing, leaving, and returning allow time for Haman to realize, beg, and fall?

c. Describe the speed or rate at which Haman's judgment and execution take place.

36. Style:

a. How has the delay of revealing her identity been to Esther's advantage?

b. Describe the effectiveness of Esther quoting Haman in his plot against the Jews.

c. What crime is Haman executed for? (v. 8)

Esther Chapter 8

1. How soon after the events of chapter 7 do the opening events of chapter 8 occur? (8:1)
2. What titles of royalty are cited in verse 1, and to whom are these titles assigned?
3. What title is Haman given? (v. 1)
4. What does Xerxes give to Esther? (v. 1)

5. Who now appears before the king? (v. 1)
6. What is reported to the king about Mordecai? (v. 1)
7. What did the king give to Mordecai? (v. 2)
8. What does Esther give to Mordecai? (v. 2)
9. For what does Esther now plead with the king? (v. 3)
10. How does the king respond to Esther? (v. 4)
11. Does this action suggest a change of location? (see 5:2)
12. What does Esther now propose the king do? (8:5)
13. What emotional tone does Esther's plea convey? (v. 6)
14. To whom does the king reply? (v. 7)
15. What actions does the king say he has already taken? (v. 7)
16. What actions does he discharge to Esther and Mordecai? (v. 8)
17. With what is the edict to be sealed? (v. 8)
    a. This is the ring given by the king to Mordecai (v. 2)
    b. This is the ring previously worn by Haman (8:2; 3:10)

18. What had Haman done with his authority? (3:10–14)

19. What does Xerxes indicate about the authority of another edict? (8:8b)

20. Who supplies the information of the events that occur next? (vv. 9–17)

21. Who is summoned? (v. 9a)

22. When are these secretaries called for? (v. 9)

23. How long has it been since Esther became queen? (2:16)

    Note: It also took one year for Esther to complete her beauty treatments. (2:12)

24. When had the royal secretaries been summoned to write Haman's letter? (3:12)

25. When is the destruction order of Haman to be carried out? (3:7, 11)

26. How much time is left to get Mordecai's message to the 127 provinces?

27. How is the narrator's information in 8:9 concerning Mordecai's letter more specific than Haman's letter of 3:14?

28. Who specifically is to hear the good news of Mordecai's letter? (8:9b)

29. Describe the authoritative actions of Mordecai, and those actions that follow, in verse 10.

30. What does this edict now allow? (v. 11)

31. How does this permission for the Jews reverse Haman's edict?

    a. Compare Haman's order in 3:13.

    b. Note Esther's quote in 7:4.

    c. Observe what the Jews are permitted in 8:11.

32. Who generally had been the target of Haman's rage? (3:13)

33. Who is defended in Mordecai's letter? (8:11)

34. What were the enemies of the Jews allowed to plunder? (3:13)

35. By contrast, what are the Jews permitted to plunder? (8:11)

36. What was the day cast for Haman's pogrom against the Jews? (3:13)

37. What is the day set by Mordecai for the defense of the Jews? (8:12)

38. Compare the narrator's comment on Haman's letter in 3:14 with Mordecai's letter in 8:13.

39. How had Haman dispatched his correspondence to the provinces? (3:13)

    a. How does Mordecai dispatch his letter? (8:14)

    b. Observe how verse 14 emphasizes the actions of verse 10.

40. What does Mordecai now wear? (v. 15)

41. What had Haman wanted to wear? (6:7–8)

42. How are these colors of the kingdom similar to the trappings of the garden party? (1:6)

43. What kind of crown does Mordecai wear? (8:15)

    a. What was the one obligatory item Vashti was to wear? (1:11)

    b. What had Xerxes given to Esther? (2:17)

    c. What had Haman coveted? (6:8—it is possible to see that "crest" in the NIV may have reference to a crown, either as an adornment for the horse or for Mordecai. If for Mordecai, compare the honor of a crown given him in 6:8 to the covering of the head in shame for Haman in 6:12.)

44. Compare the emotional state of Susa at this news (8:15b) to the prior state of mourning (3:15).

45. How is this news and this time now described for the Jews? (8:16)

46. Did Mordecai's letter reach the provinces? (vv. 9, 14, 17)

47. How did the Jews respond throughout the kingdom? (v. 17)

48. How did some non-Jews respond throughout the kingdom? (v. 17)

49. Narrator:

    a. Note the speeches of characters used by the narrator in this passage.

   b. Observe the lengthy space given to the narrator's comments on the events which transpire in this chapter.

50. Characters:

   a. Who are the primary characters of action and speech in this chapter?

   b. How do their actions, clothing, and speeches shape their characters further?

   c. How specifically is Mordecai exalted or honored in this chapter?

   d. By comparison, how much attention or space is given to Esther's actions?

51. Plot:

   a. What crisis still remains for the Jews?

   b. What proposal does Esther offer?

   c. How does the king command this problem be solved?

   d. What actions are taken by Mordecai?

   e. Is the tension resolved in this chapter?

52. Setting:

   a. What is given by Xerxes to Esther, and by Esther to Mordecai?

   b. Is a change of location suggested by verse 4? Or is this court protocol?

   c. Where is Mordecai's letter sent?

d. How is the capital of Susa cast in this chapter?

53. Time:

    a. How quickly after the execution of Haman do the events of chapter 8 transpire?

    b. How is the passing of time inferred (though the writing and dispatch of a new edict occurs with haste)?

    c. How is time inferred for the dissemination of the message and the reporting back of Jewish response to the news?

    d. When is the edict written?

    e. How much time is left for the Jews to receive Mordecai's letter and to defend themselves?

54. Style:

    a. Compare and contrast chapters 3 and 8

    b. What similarities exist between these two chapters?

    c. What unique points or emphases are highlighted?

    d. How do these differences accent the characters?

Esther Chapter 9

1. How much time has lapsed between Mordecai's letter (8:9) and the setting of chapter 9? (9:1)

2. What day is depicted in verse1? (see 3:13 and 8:11–12)

3. What is carried out on this day? (9:1)

   a. See 3:12.

   b. See also 8:10.

   c. Read these in view of 8:8.

4. What was expected to happen on this date? (9:1)

5. Instead, what occurred? (v. 2)

6. How had the Jews prepared for this day? (v. 2)

7. How is the Jewish victory on this day described in relation to enemies? (v. 2)

8. Who helped the Jews? (see 1:3; 9:3)

9. Why did these leaders help the Jews? (9:3)

10. Indicate how the text describes Mordecai's prominence. (v. 4)

11. How did the Jews in the outlying provinces deal with their enemies? (v. 5)

12. What occurred in Susa that receives singular mention? (v. 6)

13. Who specifically are mentioned as having been

killed on this day in Susa? (vv. 7–10)

14. How is Haman described? (v. 10)
15. What did the Jews do with the plunder? (v. 10)
    a. What was allowed by edict? (8:11)
    b. If the allusion to the Saul story is a familiar backdrop, how is the Jewish action here in 9:10 different from Saul's failure in 1 Samuel 15?
16. Who gives the information that a report of events in Susa reaches the king? (9:11)
17. What does the king relay to Esther? (v. 12)
18. What does the king invite Esther to do? (v. 12b)
19. What does the king again promise Esther? (v. 12b)
20. What two things does Esther ask of the king? (v. 13)
21. Where specifically is the edict to apply on the second day? (v. 13)
22. How does the king respond to Esther's request? (v. 14)
23. On this second day of defense in Susa, record how many additional enemies were slain? (v. 15)
24. How many enemies had previously been counted as falling in Susa? (v. 6)
25. What specifically is reiterated about Jewish handling of the plunder? (v. 15)

26. How are the Jews responding in other areas of the Persian kingdom? (v. 16)

27. What total is reported as having fallen to the Jewish defenders? (v. 16)

28. How did Jews in the far reaches of the kingdom handle the plunder? (v. 16)

29. On what two days does the narrator reiterate these events of Jewish defense and victory occur? (v. 17)

30. In Susa the Jews defend themselves for two days, but what do they do on the third day? (v. 18)

31. How are the actions of rural Jews highlighted in verse 19?

32. How is this day celebrated? (v. 19)

33. What does Mordecai do next? (v. 20)

34. What two days does Mordecai specify for celebration? (v. 21)

35. What is the basis for this celebration? (v. 22)

36. How is celebration observed? (v. 22)

37. What is the Jewish response to Mordecai's letter? (v. 23)

38. How is the basis for this celebration summarized in verses 24–28?

    a. List Haman's résumé as indicated in verse 24.

    b. What had Haman plotted against the Jews?

c. What did he cast?

d. What is summarized about the king's actions when the plot is discovered?

e. Who was hanged on the gallows?

f. Why is this day of celebration referred to as *Purim*?

g. What did the Jews pledge to observe?

39. How is Esther's status recorded in verse 29?

40. What do Esther and Mordecai write, and why do they write? (vv. 29–31)

41. What is indicated of Mordecai's writing? (v. 30)

42. What is indicated of Esther's writing? (v. 32)

43. Narrator:

a. What information does the narrator supply throughout this passage?

b. When speeches are given, and the narrator recedes, who speaks?

44. Characters:

a. Who are the primary characters of this passage?

b. Describe Esther's role in this chapter.

c. How is Mordecai's prominence brought to center stage in chapter 9?

d. How is Haman's shame summarized?

45. Plot:

    a. What crisis comes to bear in chapter 9?

    b. How do the reports shape the sense of Jewish victory?

    c. What resolution occurs to the challenge of death and destruction?

    d. Note how this resolution is perpetually celebrated.

46. Setting:

    a. Where does the attack and Jewish defense take place?

    b. In what city are specific activities highlighted?

    c. Where are Haman's ten dead sons hanged?

    d. Where are the edicts of Esther and Mordecai likely written from?

47. Time:

    a. What day had come in this crisis moment?

    b. How many days did the fighting and defending last?

    c. When remembering and celebrating the victory of this event, what days are recalled in the celebration?

    d. How long is the celebration to be remembered among the Jews?

48. Style:

    a. Note that Haman's ten sons are already dead (vv. 7–10)

    b. Esther calls for their public display in verse 13.

    c. Observe the effect of referring to "gallows" once again (2:23; 7:9–10; 9:13)

Esther Chapter 10

1. Who now imposes tribute on the full empire? (v. 1)

2. How is this attitude toward money different from times past?

    a. See the lengthy Persian celebrations of 1:1–8.

    b. How is the king's "generosity" displayed in 2:18?

    c. What does Xerxes tell Haman in 3:11?

    d. What does the king repeatedly swear to Esther? (see for example, 5:3)

3. What is recorded in 10:2?

4. Describe Mordecai's greatness in verse 3.

5. Where is Esther in chapter 10?

6. Narrator:

    a. Who is the speaker in chapter 10?

b. Are there any speeches by characters in this chapter?

c. Comment on how the narrator summarizes the conclusion of the book.

7. Characters:

a. Who have been the three most significant characters in the whole book?

b. How many are named in chapter 10?

8. Plot:

a. Is there any new crisis introduced in chapter 10?

b. Describe the tone of the text at this point of conclusion.

9. Setting:

a. Where does the king likely remain in order to tax his kingdom?

b. Who is taxed?

c. The empire as a whole is emphasized in the reference to which annals?

10. Time:

a. What sense of time is given in chapter 10 for the taxing of the whole empire (of 127 provinces)?

b. Is there a general sense of Mordecai's ongoing positive influence in the kingdom?

11. Style:

    a. What is the effect of Esther's absence in chapter 10?

    b. How is the absence of women at the end of the story like the beginning of the narrative in 1:1–9?

Appendix 2

Framing Observations

OBSERVATIONS ARE distinguished from interpretations where the former is concerned with detecting facts and relationships within the text itself. Observations ask, "What does the text say?" while interpretations ask, "What does the text mean?" Observations intend to report, not restate, what a passage presents.

In this appendix, examples of observations are offered from Esther chapter 1 as a helpful resource to students of Scripture. These observations build from the general array of questions offered in appendix 1, and are framed with three integral elements: a statement of declaration, a discussion of the declaration, and documentation or reference(s) supporting where the finding stems from in the narrative. For sake of clarity, this third element is demonstrated in the body of discussion, with reference to the element at the end of each example.

Observations may treat one word as a study, a single phrase or verse of analysis, a detected theme, a genre-specific element, or the like. In this appendix, four select examples are offered to assist readers who are at varying stages of their own observational development, recording, and reporting. There will be overlap in the four examples; however, the focus is on specific contextual forces of literary, historical, social, and theological aspects of Esther 1.

Greater attention is given to the literary aspects of the text, particularly in view of narrative studies. Any one paragraph in the examples may suggest an area for fuller development. For now, the purpose of the examples is to help readers begin culling and presenting information from a select narrative of analysis. These examples are not a comprehensive treatment of the passage. Appendix 3 will focus solely on the detection, collection, recording, and presentation of narrative elements.

Example 1: Literary Aspects

Declaration of Finding

Esther chapter 1 is crafted in the narrative genre.

Discussion of Finding

Biblical narrative or prose integrates the elements of a narrator who tells the story; characters who serve as the actors and actresses in the drama; a plot or story line; a setting where the story transpires; elements of time; and a writing style that effectively communicates the story. Each of these elements is briefly entertained in the following discussion.

Esther chapter 1 is told by a narrator who speaks and whose presence is overtly noted (1:1–13, 21–22). Without the "felt" presence of the narrator, events and actions in this story would not be known or understood.

Male and female characters are cast in the story, though it is clear the kingdom is run by the men. Xerxes is a prominent male king (vv. 1–2); he is an extravagant monarch who revels in lengthy and repeated celebration (vv. 1–8). Other male characters of the passage include the unnamed nobles, officials, military leaders, and princes of the empire (v. 3). Named male characters include the seven eunuchs who serve the king (v. 10), as well as the king's seven named advisors (v. 14). Of this latter grouping, Memucan emerges as a noteworthy spokesperson (vv. 15–20). Actresses are by comparison minimized to one verse (v. 9) and generally referred to without name (v. 9); Vashti the queen being the singular exception. The anger and trepidation of the men in this passage (vv. 12, 16–18) overshadow the emotional makeup (if any) of the women. In the end, Queen Vashti (vv. 9, 15–17) is systematically reduced to "Vashti" only (v. 19) and denied any further access to the king.

The chapter's plot is clearly marked by a beginning, middle, and ending, respectively setting the narrative's world; a collision of forces or conflict occurs, and relative resolution tapers the tone. Setting the initial stage is the revelry of the king's two parties (vv. 1–4; vv. 5–12). Tension mounts and is almost undetected through verse 8, though verse 9 segregates the women to an indoor location. A battle of wills occurs in the silent Vashti's repudiation of Xerxes' order (v. 12), leaving an angry king seeking advice regarding the domestic disorder (v. 13). It is Memucan (v. 16) who voices concern over Vashti's example to the other women of the kingdom (v. 18) and proposes her replacement (v. 19). It is this agenda that is adopted and aired to the far reaches of the empire (vv. 20–22).

Time elements are both stated and inferred in the passage. The world of the story is cast during the Persian-Median era (v. 3). Xerxes' first banquet (v. 4) lasts six months (180 days), with another week of revelry and freely flowing wine in the headquarters of Susa (v. 5). At the end of this week, Xerxes calls for the display of Vashti (v. 11). The text indicates a meeting with the nobles (v. 13); however, no indication is stated of how long after Vashti's infraction the meeting was called. Due to the nobles' presence in Susa for the feasting (vv. 3, 5), it is assumed Xerxes cabinet was in proximity to the capitol to swiftly convene the meeting.

Enough time lapses to allow for women of the nobility to hear of Vashti's defiance (v. 18), sparking Memucan's proposal to act quickly and decisively. Verse 22 concludes with the dispatch of the edict to the empire, implying a passing of time for the writing and dissemination of the order to the 127 provinces (v. 1).

The stage for the story begins broad, focuses local, and ends with reference to the vast kingdom. Defined in numerical and spatial terms (v. 1) the expanse is accented to give a sense of the powerful. Susa is the local headquarters for the seven-day drinking bash (vv. 5–8), as well as the likely locale for the assembly of the king's advisors. The men who drink in verses 7–8 do so outdoors in lavish surroundings (vv. 5–6); whereas the single verse of female celebration is relegated to an indoor site (v. 9), a place emphasized to be the property (not of the queen) of the king. The edict determining Vashti's fate is ultimately sent to the kingdom at large in the hopes of securing each man's local space as his own kingdom (v. 22).

Stylistically, the narrator effectively casts the king and his kingdom of opulence through greater emphasis on the masculine or power elements of the empire (see the foregoing references to male prominence in the text). It is the narrator and not Vashti herself who voices protest (v. 12), leaving her "silent," though significant. The king's dilemma regarding Vashti's punishment suggests comedic proportions to this world of power; apparently there was no prior law written on how to handle such a situation (vv. 13–22). It is humorous that a queen who did not want to appear before Xerxes (v. 12) is punished by allowing her no further access to the king (v. 19). The narrator effectively tells a story of oppression ready for irony and overthrow when another is sought to be "in Vashti's place" (see v. 19). The managers of this world seek a more domesticated figure to take Vashti's place as queen, but a subtle play on words allows for the anticipation of an agent of change, "just like (the countercultural) Vashti."

Documentation

As writers record their findings in the discussion above, references to the text are made liberally and accurately. In the event students of scripture use commentaries, significant reference works, substantive texts, journals, and so forth, these sources should be properly documented as well.

Example 2: Historical Aspects

Declaration of Finding

Esther chapter 1 is set during the exilic period.

Discussion of Finding

Historical elements imply references to time and the movement of time within the narrative world. The storyteller chooses a setting during the Persian-Median (v. 2) era, when one Xerxes (Ahasuerus) reigns (v. 1). The period is one of displacement for Jews and one of power for Gentiles. The veracity of historical information is not the focus of the text; rather, the sense of historical backdrop casts the period as one of being (over) powered by others. The opening scene makes this apparent regarding the relationship between men and women in this story.

The movement of time is both apparent and inferred, marked by the specific duration of the Persian king's parties (vv. 1–8), and the action he and his counselors take in deciding Vashti's fate (vv. 13–22).

Documentation

Documentation appears throughout the body of discussion.

Example 3: Social Aspects

Declaration of Finding

A social hierarchy is present in the configuration of the kingdom, as well as in the implied relationships between men and women in this story.

Discussion of Finding

A vast kingdom (1:1), a king (v. 2) with a royal citadel headquartered in Susa (v. 2), and unnamed leaders serving under the king shape the well-framed and ordered boundaries of life in this story. The references to a male leader (v. 2) and the administrators of his kingdom are each cast in the masculine gender: nobles, officials, princes (v. 3). The generic term *people* (v. 5) may also be understood as masculine in this context.

The top-down description of the pecking order further prioritizes males over females; the former being given more attention and narrative space in the chapter by comparison to only one verse (v. 9) for the women. One other reference to women of the empire (v. 18) is from the voice of Memucan, who seeks to maintain male superiority (vv. 20, 22).

Oddly, the king can rule 127 provinces (v. 1), command the hosting of parties (vv. 2–8), and direct the drinking festivities (vv. 7–8), but he does not know what to do with an obstinate queen (v. 13). Seven eunuchs who serve the king are snubbed by one female (vv. 10–12). Seven wise men or counselors form a body leadership advising the king (vv. 13–14). They are cast as a group of higher administrative responsibility than the seven named eunuchs who serve the king (vv. 10–11). The "powerful king" is insulated between seven who serve (v. 10) and seven who advise (v. 13). In contrast to the might of a king who displays the vast wealth of his kingdom (v. 4), one "silent" woman topples his sense of control.

Documentation

Documentation appears throughout the body of discussion.

Example 4: Theological Aspects

Declaration of Finding

Direct reference to God, deity, or any religious practice is absent from Esther chapter 1.

Discussion of Finding

The text of Esther as a whole is void of any direct reference to God. Further, there are no Persian deities, theology, or acts of worship specified in this chapter. If readers are familiar with the exilic setting and story of Daniel, there may be stylistic affinity to the Babylonian deed of toasting various gods (Dan 5), and perhaps an act of desecration of the Hebrew sacred vessels (Dan 1:1–2). However, the succeeding empire of the Medes and Persians are not cast in the same vein as the Babylonians of Daniel's story (Esth 1:5–7). The only two literary affinities between these passages are the liberality of wine and the possible distance of women from men in the act of drinking (see Esth 1:1–8 and 1:9; consider the queen in Dan 5:10 arrives to the site of the drinking men from another location; the case here is not a strong one, but an element to consider).

Some connection to the elaborate description of the king's outdoor garden party (Esth 1:6) might infer reference to the Tabernacle of Israel (Exod 25–40). Caution is urged here, however, as Esther 1 does not paint the setting as one of Persian worship; rather, it is a locale of liberal revelry (vv. 5–8).

Documentation

Documentation appears throughout the body of discussion.

Appendix 3

Compiling Narrative Observations

NARRATIVE OBSERVATIONS focus on the genre-specific elements cited in appendix 2 (under the literary examples). These six features (narrator, characters, plot, setting, time, and style) do not necessarily appear in a chapter of Scripture in this particular order. These categories are not contrived, but are identified for discussion.

One suggestion for identifying these elements in a passage of study is to have either a working copy of the chapter or a note sheet for making reference to the chapter and verse, and identification of each of the narrative elements. Students can devise a coding system for ease of reference, such as N for narrator, C for characters, and so on. Setting and style both begin with the same letter, thus Se or S1 and St or S2 may help distinguish the two elements in one's notes.

Students are encouraged to cite observations in their notes, not simply restate the passage. A columnar approach may be helpful with the reference, narrative element, and personal notes recorded as in the following example:

Reference	Narrative Element	Observations
1:1	N (Narrator) T (Time) C (Character) Se (Setting)	Narrator supplies the details; overt narrator Events are set during the period of Xerxes (NIV) (or Ahasuerus in KJV). First character of the text is King Xerxes Territory of his rule is described numerically and spatially (East-to-West direction)
1:2	N T, St Se	Narrator continues Reinforces setting; may be stylistic Headquarters of Xerxes located in Susa

Notes are necessarily taken in a methodical manner for each chapter. Collection of the information seeks to demonstrate a close and accurate reading of the text. As appropriate, cross-references to themes, word repetition, and so forth, should be included. From this set of notes and research, a student may write on any one of the six narrative elements by summarizing the entire body of data culled from the chapter under analysis. Further, the book as a whole may be engaged in a more thoughtful manner by fully tracking any one of the narrative qualities (for example, a comprehensive presentation on the character development of Queen Esther, etc.). In the following example from Esther chapter 1, the narrative element of "setting," or "space," is used to illustrate a collective presentation of findings.

The Narrative Element of "Setting," or "Space," in Esther Chapter 1

The narrator's choice of select features (geographic setting, time, character relationships, etc.) creates a stage for the events of the Esther story. The exilic context of Israel's history is the setting for this narrative (2:6). Nebuchadnezzar had carried away Mordecai and his people to Babylon at the time Jeconiah was Judah's king. Ample time lapses for the Babylonians (who receive only scant mention in the text) to be overcome by the Medo-Persian empire. The Esther story reflects the season of exile, inclusive of inferring Mordecai's advancement in age, passage of time for Haddassah's (Esther's) birth, her parents' death, and her maturation into womanhood (2:6–7).

Tailoring the events from the broad to the local (chapter 1) moves readers from the larger context of the kingdom's vast configuration to the local events of celebration in Susa. The story begins by introducing the king of the Persian empire, with details offered to shape his power base (1:1; the geographic and quantitative emphases provide a sense of the kingdom's expansive Northeast-to-Southwest dimensions [India to Ethiopia] as well as the numeric strength bolstered by mention of "127 provinces"). The story then telescopes to the local headquarters in Susa.

Three years after ascending to the throne, Xerxes hosts a feast with his hierarchical administration in attendance (v. 3). The presence of these guests reinforces the theme of power (reign; vv. 1–5), the vastness of his control (inferred in the size, geography, and quantitative details of v. 1), and what appears to be a primarily male-dominated environment (reflected in the choice of masculine nouns and larger quantity of space given to the narrative setting where men drink liberally; these aspects contrast and are distanced over against females who are mentioned only briefly in v. 9).

Reminder of the king's scope of authority (vv. 1, 3) is played off the company of the kingdom's male managers at Susa (vv. 2, 3). With this local environment squarely focused, trappings of the garden party are described.

The hanging curtains, precious metals, and colored stones are decorative accoutrements more than boundary (or limit) markers. The extravagance of the party's décor (white, green, blue, and purple hangings; silver rings; pillars of marble, sockets of gold and silver; red-carpet treatment; and white-and-black marble flooring [v. 6]), along with the elaborate and unique drinking cups of gold (v. 7), may prompt recollection of Israel's tabernacle (*Mishkawn*) (Exod 25–40). This house of worship in the Exodus account specified hangings of like hue (where white fine linen was embroidered with blue, purple, and scarlet [green is not listed]; as well as silver sockets, gold rings, and the like). However, the scene of Esther 1 is a garden party of unrestricted male revelry, not a description of Persian worship practices.

The setting of Esther 1 displays some literary affinity to the drinking party of the Babylonians in Daniel 5. In this exilic story world, Daniel utters a word of judgment when his captor-monarch toasts the gods (their power base?) with cups or bowls from Israel's temple complex (Dan 1:1–2; 5:1–4). The events of Esther 1, though, do not record any specific use of Israel's temple vessels. An ancient culture could conceivably manufacture cups from a precious metal. The point of the Esther passage highlights the international setting and local framework of wine consumption from unique drinking vessels, creating an important imagery for readers through indirect inference to similar settings. Equally possible, the uniqueness of each cup stages an era of technological advancement and artistic creativity sufficient enough to underscore affluence.

"Distance" also plays a significant part in the creation of the story's setting. While Vashti's feast is held in the context of the seven-day event of Xerxes' second party, readers are left to wonder if women had been part of the 180-day event (1:4). Readers do not hear any prohibition against women entering the king's presence until 2:14 (unless they are called for by name). Yet this is the setting of 1:10–11 where emphasis is placed on the presence of the male members and their freedom to enjoy wine without restriction. Esther 2:14 hints at the queen-wife's relationship with her husband-king; however, the concerns of chapter 4 extend to address the ban on indiscriminate female audience with the king. If these aspects found later in the text of Esther are at all incipient in chapter 1, the detail that Vashti and her female company are relegated to the limits of the royal house (belonging to the king) suggests marginalization (1:9). The subjugation is amplified in the absence of extensive details for the ladies' gathering place; for the men, a garden with elaborate frills is described, but the house for the women is given no concrete image. The only reminder offered (and that to make the point) is that the house belongs, not to the queen, but to the king.

The narrator consciously does not transition to another day or court setting for deliberation on Vashti's challenge to the king's order (v. 13). Convening a meeting with the king's seven top advisors so quickly underscores the availability of the king's "legal" council. The immediate gathering of the quorum without delay accents the point at how quickly the men move to secure their control. Enough time has lapsed for the woman of the nobility to hear of Vashti's actions (v. 19). The expediency with which the advisors decide the queen's case echoes the urgent attention given to her affront, setting the decision-making process in a male-dominated scene. Further, Memucan's immediate suggestion notes little to no delay when asked for a proposal on how to deal with the rebel queen. An edict is sent to the 127 provinces (vv. 1, 22), ending the chapter on a spatial note describing the "territorial markings," similar to how the passage began (v. 1).

Charts

The chart below is my analysis of the story's form. At chapter 4, turnabout begins as features occur in reverse order. Key: V= read column top to bottom; ^ = from bottom to top; * = element of reversal.

A.1

Feature	CH 1–2 V	CH 3 V	CH 4: Story Inverts ^	CH 5 ^
Revelry	Kingdom secure & advanced Wine feast	Haman promoted Seated at wine	No revelry—Fasting*	Haman has glad heart
Require-ment	Vashti to come Servants remind	Haman to be honored Servants remind	Jews to die under edict Mordecai reminds Esther Esther com-mands fasting	King & Haman to come to wine feast; Reiterated in dialogue
Refusal	Vashti does not come	Mordecai does not bow	Mordecai refuses	Invitation*
Reaction	King wroth	Haman angry	Esther sends raiment	King accepts

Response	Vashti to be removed Edict	Mordecai to be removed Edict	Mordecai grieves	Queen visits king
Reference	A day new queen selected	A day Jews will be attacked	News reaches gate	Three days later

A.2

Feature	CH 6: Inversion Cont. ^	CH 7: Order Returns V	CH 8: Inversion ^	CH 9–10: Inversion ^
Revelry	Mordecai honored	Wine feast	City glad	Holiday Jewish celebration
Require-ment	Haman to carry out suggestion	Queen pleads for life	Written edict sent Hierarchy to remind all	Jews permit-ed to defend themselves
Refusal	Haman does not tell real plan	Haman does not speak	Accepts Esther*	Haman's line ended
Reaction	King to honor Mordecai	King an-gry with Haman	Plans to stop pogrom	Fear fell on all
Response	King has chronicles read	Orders Haman's death	King honors Esther and Mordecai	Defense
Reference	Evening of no sleep	Haman dies that day	Day that Haman dies	Kingdom secure A day king taxed

B.

Esther: A Model for Christian Education	Confrontations With Text	Wrestles With Meaning	Acts/Moves in Solidarity
Johns and Bridges-Johns	Searching Scriptures	Yielding to the Spirit	Responding to Call
Barth	Declaration (Proclamation)	Exposition (Explication)	Address (Application)
Wells	Confession	Reflection on Confession	Ethics Grounded in Confession and Reflection
Land	Knowing	Being	Doing
Dash, Jackson, and Rasor	Liberating Encounter	Liberating Reflection	Liberating Action
Butler* (from Dash text)	What We know	What We Feel	What We Do
Edge	Knowledge Aim	Inspiration Aim	Conduct Aim

Bibliography

Adam, A. K. M. *What is Postmodern Biblical Criticism?* Minneapolis: Augsburg Fortress, 1995.

Adeney, Miriam. "Esther Across Cultures: Indigenous Leadership Roles for Women." *Missiology* 15, no. 3 (1987) 323–37.

Alter, Robert. *The Art of Biblical Narrative.* New York: Basic, 1981.

Amit, Yairah. *Reading Biblical Narratives.* Minneapolis: Augsburg Fortress, 2001.

Archer, Kenneth J. "Pentecostal Hermeneutics and a Critique of the Evangelical Historical-Critical Method." Conference paper, Evangelical Theological Society, 2002.

Bach, Alice. "Mirror, Mirror in the Text: Reflections on Reading and Rereading." In *A Feminist Companion to Esther, Judith, and Susanna*, 81-86. Sheffield, England: Sheffield Academic, 1995.

Bal, Mieke. "Lots of Writing." *Semeia* 54, no. 1 (1991) 77–102.

Bar-Efrat, Shimon. *Narrative Art in the Bible.* Sheffield, England: Sheffield Academic, 1997.

Barna, George. "Christians Say They Do Best at Relationships, Worst in Bible Knowledge." June 14, 2005. No pages. Accessed June 29, 2007. Online: http://www.barna.org/Flex Page.aspx? Page= BarnaUpdate&BarnaUpdateID=190.

Barth, Karl. "The Task of the Community." *The Doctrine of Reconciliation.* Church Dogmatics, vol. 4, part 3, second half. Edingburgh: T & T Clark, 1962.

Bartholomew, Craig, Colin Green, and Karl Moller. *Renewing Biblical Interpretation.* Grand Rapids: Zondervan, 2000.

Beal, Timothy K. "Tracing Esther's Beginnings." In *A Feminist Companion to Esther, Judith. and Susanna*, 87–110. Sheffield, England: Sheffield Academic, 1995.

Bechtel, Carol M. *Esther.* Louisville: John Knox, 2000

Berlin, Adele. "The Role of the Text in the Reading Process." *Semeia* 62 (1993) 143–47.

———. "The Book of Esther and Ancient Storytelling." *Journal of Biblical Literature* 120, no. 1 (Spring 2001) 3–14.

Brenner, Athalya. "Looking at Esther Through the Looking Glass." In *A Feminist Companion to Esther, Judith, and Susanna*, 71–80. Sheffield, England: Sheffield Academic, 1995.

———. "Who's Afraid of Feminist Criticism? Who's Afraid of Biblical Humor? The Case of the Obtuse Foreign Ruler in the Hebrew Bible." *Journal for the Study of the Old Testament* 63, no.1 (1994) 38–55.

Bridges-Johns, Cheryl. *Finding Eternal Treasures*. Cleveland, TN: Pathway, 1986.

———. *Pentecostal Formation: Pedagogy Among the Oppressed*. Sheffield, England: Sheffield Academic, 1991.

Briggs, Richard. *Reading the Bible Wisely*. Grand Rapids: Baker Academic, 2003.

Bronner, Leila Leah. "Esther Revisited: An Aggadic Approach." In *A Feminist Companion to Esther, Judith, and Susanna*, 176–97. Sheffield, England: Sheffield Academic, 1995.

Brown, William. *Character in Crisis*. Grand Rapids: Eerdmans, 1996.

Brueggemann, Walter. *Message of the Psalms*. Minneapolis: Augsburg Fortress, 1984.

———. *Theology of the Old Testament*. Minneapolis: Augsburg Fortress, 1997.

Campbell, Edward F. "Relishing the Bible as Literature and History." *The Christian Century* 109 (1992) 812–15.

Childs, Brevard. "War with the Amalekites: 17:8–16." In *The Book of Exodus: A Critical Theological Commentary*, 310–17. Philadelphia: Westminster, 1974.

Clines, David J. A. "In Quest of the Historical Mordecai." *Vestus Testamentum* 41, no. 2 (1991) 129–36.

———. "Story and Poem: The Old Testament as Literature and as Scripture." *Interpretation* 34, no. 2 (1980) 115–27.

Copenhaver, Martin B. "A Conspiracy of Deliverance." *The Christian Century* 111, no. 25, S 7–14 (1994) 811.

Craig, Kenneth M. Jr. *Reading Esther: A Case for the Literary Carnivalesque*. Louisville: Westminster John Knox, 1995.

Dash, Michael I. N., Jonathan Jackson, and Stephen C. Rasor. *Hidden Wholeness: An African-American Spirituality for Individuals and Communities*. Cleveland: Pilgrim, 1997.

De Troyer, Kristin. "An Oriental Beauty Parlor: An Analysis of Esther 2:8–18 in the Hebrew, the Septuagint and the Second Greek

Text." In *A Feminist Companion to Esther, Judith, and Susanna*, 47–70. Sheffield, England: Sheffield Academic, 1995.

Dillard, Raymond B., and Tremper Longman. *An Introduction to the Old Testament.* Grand Rapids: Zondervan, 1994.

Duvall, J. Scott, and J. Daniel Hayes. *Grasping God's Word. 2d ed.* Grand Rapids: Zondervan, 2005.

Edge, Findley. *Teaching for Results.* Nashville: Broadman & Holman, 1995.

Fee, Gordon, and Douglas Stewart. *How to Read the Bible for All It's Worth.* Grand Rapids: Zondervan, 1984.

Fewell, Dana Nolan. *Circle of Sovereignty: Plotting Politics in the Book of Daniel.* Nashville: Abingdon, 1991.

Fewell, Dana Nolan, and David M. Gunn. *Narrative in the Hebrew Bible.* New York: Oxford UP, 1993.

Florence, Anna Carter. "The Woman Who Just Said 'No.'" *Journal for Preachers* (1998) 37–40.

Fox, Michael V. *Character and Ideology in the Book of Esther.* Columbia: University of South Carolina, 1991.

Fuchs, Esther. "For I Have the Way of Women: Deception, Gender, and Ideology in Biblical Narrative." *Semeia* 42, no. 1 (1988) 68–83.

Gitay, Zefira. "Esther and the Queen's Throne." In *A Feminist Companion to Esther, Judith, and Susanna*, 136–48. Sheffield, England: Sheffield Academic, 1995.

Glustrom, Simon. *The Language of Judaism.* New Jersey: Jason Aronson, Inc., 1986.

Goldingay, John. "Biblical Story and the Way It Shapes Our Story." *The Journal of the European Pentecostal Theological Association* 17 (1997) 5–15.

———. *Israel's Gospel*, vol. 1. Downers Grove, IL: Intervarsity, 2003.

Goldman, Stan. "Narrative and Ethical Ironies in Esther." *Journal for the Study of the Old Testament* 47, no. 1 (1990) 15–31.

Gonzalez, Justo L. *Santa Biblia: The Bible Through Hispanic Eyes.* Nashville: Abingdon, 1996.

Gordis, Robert. "Religion, Wisdom and History in the Book of Esther: A New Solution to an Ancient Crux." *Journal of Biblical Literature* 100 (1981) 359–88.

Groome, Thomas H. *Christian Religious Education.* San Francisco: Harper San Francisco, 1980.

Guthmann, Sidney. "Passover: The Past in the Present." *The Journal of Religion and Physical Research* (July 2002): 122–23.

Hallo, William W. "The First Purim." *Biblical Archaeologist* 46, no. 1 (1983) 19–26.

Hambrick-Stowe, Charles E. "Ruth the New Abraham, Esther the New Moses." *Christian Century* 100, no. 37 (1983) 1130–34.

Harvey, Van A. *A Handbook of Theological Terms*. New York: MacMillan, 1964.

Heibert, Frances F. "Finding Favor: A Missionary Orientation." *Missiology* 17, no. 2 (1989) 143–57.

Henrichsen, Walter, and Gayle Jackson. *Studying, Interpreting, and Applying the Bible*. Grand Rapids: Zondervan, 1990.

Hoerth, Alfred J., Gerald L. Mattingly, and Edwin M. Yamauchi. *Peoples of the Old Testament World*. Grand Rapids: Baker, 1994.

House, Paul R. *Old Testament Theology*. Downers Grove, IL: InterVarsity, 1988.

Humphreys, W. Lee. "The Story of Esther in Its Several Forms: Recent Studies." *Religious Studies Review* 24, no. 4 (1988) 335–42.

Jeffers, A. Review of *Ruth and Esther: A Feminist Companion to the Bible*, 2d ser., by Athalaya Brenner, *Journal for the Study of the Old Testament* 89, no. 01 (2000) 69–70.

Johns, Jackie David, and Cheryl Bridges-Johns. "Yielding to the Spirit." *Journal of Pentecostal Theology* no. 1 (1992) 109–34.

Jones, Bruce W. "Two Misconceptions about the Book of Esther." *Catholic Biblical Quarterly* 39, no. 2 (1997) 171–81.

Kallai, Zecharia. "Biblical Historiography and Literary History: A Programmatic Survey." *Vestus Testamentum* 49, no. 3 (1999) 338–50.

Keil, C. F., and Franz Delitzsch. "Esther." *Commentary on the Old Testament*, vol. 3, Peabody, MA: Hendrickson, 1989.

Klein, Lillian R. "Honor and Shame in Esther." In *A Feminist Companion to Esther, Judith, and Susanna*, 149–75. Sheffield, England: Sheffield Academic, 1995.

Kolatch, Alfred J. *The Jewish Book of Why*. New York: Jonathan David, 1981.

Laffey, Alice L. Review of *Reading Esther: A Case for the Literary Carnivalesque*, by Kenneth M. Craig Jr. *The Catholic Biblical Quarterly* 59, no. 2 (1997) 342.

La Sor, William S., David A. Hubbard, and Fredric W. Bush. *Old Testament Survey: The Message, Form, and Background of the Old Testament*. 2d ed. Grand Rapids: Eerdmans, 1996.

Land, Steven J. *A Passion for the Kingdom: An Analysis of Pentecostal Spirituality*. Ann Arbor: UMI Dissertation Information Services, 1991.

Leigh, Ronald W. *Direct Bible Discovery*. Nashville: Broadman, 1982.

Levenson, Jon D. *Esther*. Louisville: Westminster John Knox, 1997.

———. "The Scroll of Esther in Ecumenical Perspective." *Journal of Ecumenical Studies* 13, no. 3 (1976) 440–52.

McClendon, James Wm. "More on Narrative." *Theology Today* 40 (1983) 49–53.

Mickelsen, A. Berkeley, and Alvera M. Mickelsen. *Understanding Scripture: How to Read and Study the Bible*. Peabody: Hendrickson, 1986.

Mitchell, Pamela. "Why Care About Stories? A Theory of Narrative Art." *Religious Education* 86, no. 01 (1991) 30–43.

Mosala, Itumeleng J. "The Implications of the Text of Esther for African Women's Struggle for Liberation in South Africa." *Semeia* 59, no. 1 (1992) 129–37.

Neusner, Jacob. *The Mishnah: A New Translation*. New Haven, CT: Yale UP, 1988.

———. "Meggilah." *The Talmud of Babylonia: A Complete Outline—Part I B*. Atlanta: Scholars, 1995.

Niditch, Susan. "Esther: Folklore, Wisdom, Feminism and Authority." In *A Feminist Companion to Esther, Judith, and Susanna*, 26–46. Sheffield, England: Sheffield Academic, 1995.

Osborne, Grant R. *The Hermeneutical Spiral*. Downers Grove, IL: InterVarsity, 1991.

Pfeiffer, Charles F. "Esther and the Persian Court." In *Old Testament History*, 488–97. Grand Rapids: Baker, 1973.

Pfeiffer, Robert H. "Esther." In *The Abingdon Bible Commentary*, 477–82. New York: Doubleday, 1929.

Polish, Daniel F. "Aspects of Esther: A Phenomenological Exploration of the Megillah of Esther and the Origins of Purim." *Journal for the Study of the Old Testament* 85 (1999) 85–106.

Richards, Lawrence, and Gary Bredfeldt. *Creative Bible Teaching*. Chicago: Moody, 1998.

Rosenblatt, Naomi Harris. "Portraits of Heroism: Esther and Samson." *Bible Review.*15 (February 1999) 20–25, 47. (See also *Bible Review: The Archive 1985–2003*: F 15 line 49).

Ryken, Leland. *How to Read the Bible as Literature*. Grand Rapids: Zondervan, 1984.

Sailhammer, John H. *Introduction to Old Testament Theology: A Canonical Approach*. Grand Rapids: Zondervan, 1995.

———. *The Pentateuch as Narrative*. Grand Rapids: Zondervan, 1992.

Schurer, Emil. *A History of the Jewish People in the Time of Jesus Christ*, second division, vol. 3. Peabody: Hendrickson, 1994.

Scullion, John J. "Marchen, Sage, Legende: Towards a Clarification of Some Literary Terms Used by Old Testament Scholars." *Vestus Testamentum* 34, no. 3 (1984) 321–36.

Segovia, Fernando F. *Decolonizing Biblical Studies: A View From the Margins*. Mary Knoll, NY: Orbis, 2000.

Stone, Howard W., and James O. Duke. *How to Think Theologically*, 2d ed. Minneapolis: Augsburg Fortress, 2006.

Talmon, S. "Wisdom in the Book of Esther." *Vestus Testamentum* 13, no. 4 (1963) 419–55.

Van Wijk-Bos, Johanna W. H. *Ruth and Esther: Women in Alien Lands*. Nashville: Abingdon, 2001.

Vermes, Geza. *The Complete Dead Sea Scrolls in English*. New York: Penguin, 1997.

Weiland, Forrest S. "Literary Clues to God's Providence in the Book of Esther" *Bibliotheca Sacra* 160 (2003) 34–47.

Wells, David. *No Place for Truth: Or Whatever Happened to Evangelical Theology?* Grand Rapids: Eerdmans, 1993.

Wenham, Gordon J. "The Coherence of the Flood Narrative." *Vestus Testamentum* 28, no. 03 (1978) 336–48.

Whiston, William. "Concerning Esther, and Mordecai, and Haman: And How in the Reign of Artaxerxes, the Whole Nation of the Jews Was in Danger of Perishing." *The Works of Josephus: Complete and Unabridged*. Antiquities 11.6.1–13; 1987.

Wiebe, John M. "Esther 4:14: Will Relief and Deliverance Arise for the Jews From Another Place?" *The Catholic Biblical Quarterly* 53, no. 3 (1991) 409–15.

Wolkstein, Diane. "Esther's Story." In *A Feminist Companion to Esther, Judith, and Susanna*, 198–206. Sheffield, England: Sheffield Academic, 1995.

Wood, Ralph C. "People Are Funny." *Christian Century* 114, no. 29 (1997) 975–76.

Wyler, Bea. "Esther: The Incomplete Emancipation of a Queen." *A Feminist Companion to Esther, Judith, and Susanna*, 111–35. Sheffield, England: Sheffield Academic, 1995.

Yamauchi, Edwin M. "Mordecai, the Persepolis Tablets, and the Susa Excavations." *Vestus Testamentum* 42, no. 2 (1992) 272–75.

Other Resources

The following references have not been cited in the body of the paper; they are, however, included here as additional resource material for the interested reader. These works include reviews of texts cited in this book, as well as other aspects of narrative studies designed to broaden the reading interests of students.

Archer, Kenneth J. "Early Pentecostal Biblical Interpretation: Blurring the Boundaries." Conference paper presented at the 29th Annual Meeting of the Society for Pentecostal Studies, Kirkland, Washington, 2000.

———. "Pentecostal Babblings: The Narrative Hermeneutic of the Marginalized." Conference paper presented at the 27th Annual Meeting of the Society for Pentecostal Studies in Special Session with the Wesleyan Theological Society, 1998.

Bandstra, Barry L. *Reading the Old Testament: An Introduction to the Hebrew Bible*. 2d ed. Belmont: Wadsworth, 1999.

Benin, Stephen D. Review of *Esther in Medieval Garb: Jewish Interpretation of the Book of Esther in the Middle Ages*, by Barry Dov Walfish." *Religious Studies Review* 20, no. 4, (1994) 346.

Bergant, Dianne. Review of *From Eve to Esther: Rabbinic Reconstructions of Biblical Women*, by Leila Leah Bronner. *Catholic Biblical Quarterly* 58, no. 2. (1996) 341–42.

Brooks, Keith L. *Basic Bible Study*. Chicago: Moody, 1961.

Brueggemann, Walter. Review of *The Esther Scroll: The Story of the Story*, by David Clines. *Interpretation* 40, no. 2 (1986) 202.

———. "Truth Telling as Subversive Obedience." *Journal for Preachers* 25, no. 2 (1997) 2–9.

Burns, Camilla. Review of *Reading Esther: A Case for the Literary Carnivalesque*, by Kenneth M. Craig, Jr. *Theological Studies* 57, no 3 (1996) 564.

Craig, Kenneth M. Jr. Review of *The Esther Scroll: The Story of the Story*, by David Clines. *Journal of Biblical Literature* 106, no. 01 (1987) 118–19.

Crawford, Sidnie White. "Esther Not Judith." *Bible Review* 18, no. 1 (2002) 21–31, 45.

———. Review of *Esther: A Commentary*, by Jon D. Levenson. *Journal of Biblical Literature* 118, no. 1 (1999) 134–36.

———. Review of *The Alpha-Text of Esther: Its Character and Relationship to the Masoretic Text*, by Karen H. Jobes." *Catholic Biblical Quarterly* 60, no. 4 (1998) 735–36.

———. Review of *Three Faces of a Queen: Characterization in the Book of Esther*, by Linda Day. *Catholic Biblical Quarterly* 59, no. 1 (1997) 114–15.

Day, Linda. Review of *Esther: A Theological Approach*, by Angel Manuel Rodriquez. *Catholic Biblical Quarterly* 58, no. 4 (1996) 721–22.

———. Review of *Esther: A Commentary*, by Jon D. Levenson. *The Catholic Biblical Quarterly* 60 (1998) 534–35.

———. Review of *Reading Esther: A Case for the Literary Carnivalesque*, by Kenneth M. Craig Jr. *Journal of Biblical Literature* 117, no. 2 (1998) 346–48.

Dell, Katherine J. Review of "Character and Ideology in the Book of Esther" by Michael V. Fox. *Vestus Testamentum* 46, no. 4 (1996) 572–73.

Ellington, Scott A. "History, Story, and Testimony: Locating Truth in a Pentecostal Hermeneutic." Conference paper presented at the 29th Annual Meeting of the Society for Pentecostal Studies, Kirkland, Washington, 2000.

Fried, Lisbeth S. "Toward the Ur-Text of Esther." *Journal for the Study of the Old Testament* 88 (2000) 49–57.

Golomb, David M. Review of *The Two Targums of Esther*, by Bernard Grossfeld. *The Catholic Biblical Quarterly* 56, no. 1 (1994) 108–9.

Gunn, David M. Review of *The Art of Biblical Narrative*, by Robert Alter. *Journal for the Study of the Old Testament*. 29, no. 1 (1984) 109–16.

Hess, Carol Lackey. *Caretakers of our Common House: Women's Development in Communities of Faith*. Nashville: Abingdon, 1997.

Hester, H. I. "Queen Esther." In *The Heart of Hebrew History: A Study of the Old Testament*. 42d printing, 263–365. Liberty: Quality, 1962.

Hill, Andrew E. and John H. Walton. "Esther." In *A Survey of the Old Testament*, 238–43 Grand Rapids: Zondervan, 1991.

Horbury, William. "The Name Mardochaeus in a Ptolemaic Inscription." *Vestus Testamentum* 41, no. 2 (1991) 220–26.

Jenson, Robert W. "How the World Lost Its Story." *First Things* 36 (1993) 19–24.

Jones, Bruce William. Review of *The Esther Scroll: The Story of the Story*, by David Clines. *The Catholic Biblical Quarterly* 48, no. 04 (1986) 712–14.

LaCocque, Andre. Review of *Character and Ideology in the Book of Esther*, by Michael V. Fox. *Interpretation* 47, no. 2 (1993) 188–89.

Lipton, Diana. Review of *Esther: A Theological Approach*, by Angel Manuel Rodriguez. *Vestus Testamentum* 47, no. 4 (1997) 565–66.

Longman, Tremper. *How to Read the Psalms*. Downers Grove, IL: InterVarsity, 1998.

McLay, Tim. Review of *The Alpha-Text of Esther: Its Character and Relationship to the Masoretic Text*, by Karen H. Jobes. *Journal of Biblical Literature* 118, no. 4 (1999) 724–26.

Moore, Carey A. "Archaeology and the Book of Esther." *The Biblical Archaeologist* 38, no. 304, (1975) 62–79.

———. Review of *The Redaction of the Books of Esther*, by Michael V. Fox. *The Catholic Biblical Quarterly* 55, no. 2, (1993) 334–35.

Murphy, Roland E. Review of *Character and Ideology in the Book of Esther*, by Michael V. Fox. *The Catholic Biblical Quarterly* 55, no. 2 (1993) 333–34.

Newsom, Carol A. Review of *Character and Ideology in the Book of Esther*, by Michael V. Fox. *Journal of the American Academy of Religion* 63, no. 3 (1995) 618–21.

Palmer, Parker. *The Courage to Teach*. San Francisco: Jossey-Bass, 1988.

Reid, Stephen B. Review of *Ezra, Nehemiah and Esther (The Daily Study)*, by J. G. McConville. *The Catholic Biblical Quarterly* 50, no. 2 (1988) 301–2.

Savran, George. *Telling and Retelling: Quotation in Biblical Narrative*. Bloomington: Indiana UP. 1988.

Schultz, Samuel J. "The Story of Esther." *The Old Testament Speaks*. 3d ed. San Francisco: Harper and Row, 1980.

Seitz, Christopher R. Review of *Israel Among the Nations: A Commentary on the Books of Nahum and Obadiah and Esther (International Theological Commentary)*, by Richard J. Coggins and S. Paul Re'emi. *The Catholic Biblical Quarterly* 50, no. 1 (1988) 122–23.

Seymour, Jack L., and Donald E. Miller. *Contemporary Approaches to Christian Education*. Nashville: Abingdon, 1982.

Smith, James K. A. *The Fall of Interpretation: Philosophical Foundations for a Creational Hermeneutic*. Downers Grove, IL: InterVarsity, 2000.

Smith-Christopher, Daniel. Review of *Ezra, Nehemiah, Esther* (The New American Commentary), by Mervin Breneman. *The Catholic Biblical Quarterly* 57, no. 1 (1995) 118–20.

Smothers, Thomas G. Review of *The Esther Scroll: The Story of the Story*, by David Clines. *Review and Expositor* 87, no. 3 (1990) 490–91.

Stackhouse, John G. Jr. "Finding a Home for Eve." *Christianity Today* (1999) 60–61.

Throntveit, Mark A. Review of *Ezra, Nehemiah, and Esther*, by Johanna W. H. Van Wijk-Bos." *Interpretation* 53, no. 4 (1999) 422.

Vos, Howard. *Effective Bible Study*. Grand Rapids: Zondervan, 1956.

Vrudny, Kimberly. "Medieval Fascination with the Queen: Esther as the Queen of Heaven and Host of the Messianic Banquet." *The Arts in Theological Studies* 11, no. 2 (1999) 36–43.

Wechsler, Michael G. "The Purim-Passover Connection: A Reflection of Jewish Exegetical Tradition in the Peshitta Book of Esther." *Journal of Biblical Literature* 117, no. 2 (1998) 321–27.

White, Sidnie Ann. Review of *The Redaction of the Books of Esther: On Reading Composite Texts*, by Michael V. Fox. *Journal of Biblical Literature* 112, no. 1 (1993) 139–40.

Wright, John W. Review of *Character and Ideology in the Book of Esther*, by Michael V. Fox." *Journal of Biblical Literature* 112, no. 1 (1993) 140–42.

www.ingramcontent.com/pod-product-compliance
Lightning Source LLC
La Vergne TN
LVHW010931100826
845153LV00001B/2

* 9 7 8 1 4 9 8 2 5 0 6 7 2 *